For All Time?

For All Time?

CRITICAL ISSUES IN
TEACHING SHAKESPEARE

Edited by

Paul Skrebels and Sieta van der Hoeven

**Wakefield
Press**

Wakefield Press
17 Rundle Street
Kent Town
South Australia 5067

in association with

The Australian Association for the Teaching of English
416 Magill Road
Kensington Gardens
South Australia 5068

First published 2002

AATE Interface Series Commissioning Editor, Sieta van der Hoeven

Cover design by Dean Lahn, Lahn Stafford Design
Text design and typesetting by Clinton Ellicott
Printed and bound by Hyde Park Press

National Library of Australia
Cataloguing-in-publication entry

For all time?: critical issues in teaching Shakespeare.

Bibliography.
Includes index.
ISBN 1 86254 595 2.

1. Shakespeare, William, 1564–1616 – Study and teaching.
I. Skrebels, Paul. II. Hoeven, Sieta van der.

822.33

Contents

Foreword

John Bell AM, OBE

Artistic Director,
The Bell Shakespeare Company

Happy the person who can say (as I can): 'I had a couple of fantastic teachers in high school who taught me to love Shakespeare'. Such a claim is probably outnumbered three to one by those who say: 'You'll never drag me into a theatre to see Shakespeare – I hated it so much at school'.

When I was at school the actual method of inculcating Shakespeare was dreary enough: 'Read a line aloud then pass the book to the boy next to you …' Luckily in my case this was balanced by the enthusiasm of the teachers themselves who topped it up with expeditions to the cinema to see Olivier's *Henry V*, *Hamlet* and *Richard III*. That was where Shakespeare really came alive and set my heart on fire.

My daughters were less fortunate, encountering one of those hostile feminist teachers who made it clear how much she resented having to teach chauvinist propaganda by a dead white male.

Things got a little better in the 90s and a little worse: a little better with emphasis on Shakespeare as performance material with kids actually getting up and doing it. A little worse (at least in parts of Australia) with Shakespeare made a marginal option in many curricula, removing the opportunity of even a nodding acquaintance for many students.

But things got tougher for teachers too. I remember one asking my advice. She said 'I have just forty hours teaching time to get my class through the H.S.C. with *Antony and Cleopatra*. They're nearly all Vietnamese and can't speak English … What do I do?'

It's heartening to find a book that tackles current dilemmas from many angles and with a good deal of commitment. I was particularly struck by D. Kay Johnston and

Margaret Maurer's rationale for their chapter: 'If lack of certainty offers occasions for stimulating intellectual growth, Shakespeare's plays, particularly as they have been disrupted by late-twentieth century critical and scholarly activity, have a specific value to be included in the curricula of undergraduate and upper-secondary education. ... it is that dual aspect of respectability and susceptibility to provocative disruption that makes Shakespeare particularly valuable to the learning of students and professional development of teachers.'[1]

It is also heartening to find some educationalists who can lift their visions beyond pedagogy to remind us of the sheer pleasure of Shakespeare's theatre, the aesthetic and moral achievement of his work. Speaking of *The Rape of Lucrece*, Mary Janell Metzger proposes that 'that the historical yet poetic nature of the poem's representation of Lucrece functions to teach students the danger of absolutism – literary or political – and the ways in which the creative use of language can work to enlarge our feelings for the moral complexity of the world and the role of feeling in discerning truth within it'.

In 'Studying the Art of Provoking' Pavel Drábek shows a fine sensitivity in appreciating the dramatist's skills of structure, storytelling and sheer theatricality, while Derek Peat, talking about the value of performance says: 'My own teaching of Shakespeare has always been informed by the belief that students learn best by working with the text through performance. If this is done under something approximating "original" performance conditions, it can lead quite naturally into an exploration of performances through time and of the ways in which audiences may value and respond.'

In my own experience, once students understand the meaning of the words, the power of uttering them is a heady and transporting experience. They find that Shakespeare taps into emotions and scenarios that are recognisable and familiar to adolescents. Moreover, his characters mean what they say. The lack of 'subtext' makes for an invigorating candour and purity of expression that can be intensely moving.

Perhaps the aims and value of this publication are best summarised by John Joughin when he says that 'the survival of Shakespeare inside and outside the classroom is caught up in a process which is interruptive, untimely and out-of-joint. This means that each encounter is singular, always a first time as well as a last time ... In this sense at least, then, teaching and theorising Shakespeare cannot be part of some universal or "never ending" process. Indeed, for most of us it can only ever be said to have just begun'.

J. B.

Notes

1 The quotations in this foreword were taken from the authors' proposals, and do not necessarily appear verbatim in the chapters that follow.

Introduction

Exactly twenty years ago, in an essay forming part of a ground-breaking collection called *Re-Reading English*, Derek Longhurst investigated the place of Shakespeare in the British curriculum with a view to making explicit how his work 'has been used, especially since the 1920s, to construct and justify dominant conceptions of a literary education' (1982: 150). Cleverly inverting Ben Jonson's praise of the Bard to read 'Not for all time, but for an Age', Longhurst's essay sought to re-historicise the processes by which 'Shakespeare's plays are given overwhelming priority' (1982: 154) in both the teaching of English and 'comprehensive' education generally. Primarily, the essay investigated the parts played by Leavis, Knights, Tillyard and other 'big name' critics of the early- to mid-twentieth century in building upon Matthew Arnold's concepts of the moral value of literature to inform the newly-emerging English curriculum.

Statements such as 'the ideological power of culture rests on a definition of "great literature" as "timeless", "eternal", "universal"' – here Longhurst is quoting from the 1921 Newbolt Report, *The Teaching of English in England* – 'and Shakespeare is used continually to prove it' (1982: 151), and an agenda that includes 'introducing [students] to the notion that "Literature" has been constituted by the criticism which "reads it"' (1982: 160), locate Longhurst's work as an early foray into the field of Cultural Studies. This latter discipline, variously vilified by literary 'purists' as interfering in, corrupting, or merely irrelevant to the study of literature, has perhaps more than any other over the last two decades redefined our approach to that 'thing' we call literature. Twenty years is at once a very short span of human history yet long enough for a culture itself to change markedly. We have moved in that time from a rather hard-to-adequately-define Post-Industrial Era to a much more obvious Age of Information; in terms of the gigabytes of material available to us through a multiplicity of media, Shakespeare is in danger of being perceived as just another set of data to be stored and (perhaps) eventually retrieved. The issue is becoming one of encouraging teachers and students to do more than just retrieve the data.

During the decade following the efforts of Longhurst and others to open up the territory, Literary Studies scholars began picking up on the observations of their Cultural Studies colleagues about how 'the modernist world of certainty ... has given way to a shared postmodern culture in which representational borders collapse into new hybridised forms of cultural performance, identity, and political agency' (Giroux 1994: 288). Thus Antony Easthope, in developing his program of *Literary into Cultural Studies* (1991), saw it as no longer possible for teachers to treat a text as 'a self-defining object' to which they must lead students with reverence and awe (1991: 12). Instead, taking their cue from the post-structuralist theories at the core of Cultural Studies, teachers should provide opportunities for texts and students (as readers, viewers, consumers, in whatever mode of reception) to 'interact dialectically' (1991: 21).

Hence, twenty years on, the present collection, framed by the same concern as Longhurst's, but reconfigured into the slightly less certain interrogatory form, 'For all time?' Certainly in some educational systems Shakespeare is no longer a compulsory element of the English syllabus, although his work still represents a cornerstone of our cultural capital, as any mainstream theatre company that fails to include at least one Shakespeare play in its season of works is likely to discover. And one need only think of the number of recent commercially produced Shakespeare films, whether 'straight' à la Branagh, almost unrecognisably adapted as in *Ten Things I Hate about You*, or somewhere in between the two with Luhrmann's *Romeo+Juliet*, to realise how readily the Bard's cultural capital can still be converted into the monetary kind. So, while one hesitates to say 'whether they like it or not', teachers of English at secondary and tertiary levels still need to bring their students and Shakespeare face-to-face at some stage in each others' careers.

The collection presented here demonstrates two other aspects of the process. First, that there are many teachers committed to finding ways of achieving this meeting out of a love for the material and a commitment to the inherent value of exposure to Shakespeare. And second, that this process is framed in the kinds of methodologies that reveal the disjuncture between 'theorised' tertiary study and 'untheorised' secondary education to be no longer as pronounced as it may have been in the earlier days of the move to a more culturally-oriented criticism. Secondary teachers have almost always sought ways of making Shakespeare 'relevant' to their less captive audiences; the methods dealt with in a collection such as this will at least refute any claims that what they have been doing is somehow tangential to or 'isn't really' literary study. We trust that these chapters provide a satisfactory mix of theory and practice (or rather, of *praxis*, or theorised practice); we offer them in the belief that theory not grounded in practice is of little value to the overworked teacher, while practice without theory can degenerate into 'busy work' on the one hand, or, worse, can operate on the pretence that what is being done in class is somehow 'above' or 'beyond' ideology, which is probably the most sinister ideological stance of all. We are certain that there is something here of interest to all teachers of Shakespeare, and indeed of literature generally at the secondary and tertiary education levels, and that they will be stimulated to consider the relevance of the ideas and practices described here to their own work.

That educational institutions are not simply repositories of the canon of English literature but are instrumental in devising, perpetuating and reshaping it is an important point of departure for considering the continued place of Shakespeare in the curriculum. As Robert Eaglestone puts it plainly, 'A person who studied English and has become a teacher often teaches the texts that he or she was taught, in part because she or he was taught that these texts were the most important' (2000: 56). Mark Houlahan's chapter in this collection, 'Shakespeare, Hegemony and Assessment in New Zealand High Schools', while dealing with a specific cultural experience, nevertheless adequately demonstrates the power that examination bodies anywhere have for not only defining but actually delimiting the Shakespeare canon, and that the influence such bodies exert has wide-ranging and long-lasting consequences. 'Exposing Shakespeare: Introducing English Studies at University' by Catherine Silverstone (also a New Zealander, but teaching and studying in the UK), also reveals how, by using Shakespeare as much as a means for introducing students to literary critical practice as for his own sake, a university course might also take for granted Shakespeare's centrality to the canon. Even so, she proposes ways for developing this assumption into a means of exploring key issues in rethinking the design of literary studies courses at the tertiary level for the new millennium.

In 'An Approach to Teaching Shakespeare: *King Lear* and the New Senior English Syllabus in New South Wales', Derek Peat also takes advantage of a time of change, in which the notion of 'text' has been broadened to include much more than just the 'play-on-the-page', to apply and develop his own ideas about teaching Shakespeare through practical dramatic methods. Ted Tibbetts' 'Teaching Shakespeare through Performance' tackles the same methodology but at a more general level, in the conviction that using performance techniques to teach Shakespearean texts satisfies the requirements of 'best teaching practice' to be 'authentic, engaging, and student-centred'[1] Roger Ochse takes the practical approach several steps further into the future of mediated texts in 'Digital Shakespeare: Integrating Texts and Technology'. He discusses ways of creating 'a coordinated triangular approach' that melds the language, performance history and students' own reinterpretations of Shakespeare through the use of digital audio and visual technology.

An emphasis on practical activities in teaching Shakespeare by no means precludes a consideration of theory, however. It is, after all, a premise of this collection that the two are essentially interdependent. The capacity for practice and theory to coexist in the Shakespeare class is at the core of my own chapter, 'Shakespeare Reworked: Textual Intervention Strategies in a University Writing Classroom', where a particular 'hands on' pedagogy for making meaning from Shakespeare texts is explained in terms of some recent ideas about sharing around cultural capital and using some actual student examples to illustrate how this might be achieved. Similarly, the notion that Shakespeare's work can both generate new texts and may in turn be read alongside or even against such reworkings is the concern of Mary Christel's 'Teaching *The Tempest*: One Tale, Many Texts'. This chapter suggests some ways that a potentially complex critical issue like postcolonialism, and the multiple readings and interpretations such an approach has generated, might be introduced at the secondary education level. Mary J. Metzger's 'To "See Feelingly": Reading Shakespeare's *The Rape of Lucrece*' tackles both a difficult issue and a little-used work, as she relates the ways in which she and her college class dealt with the poem and its relevance to their own lives, particularly in its capacity as 'a powerful vehicle for exploring the role of individual action in the creation of social justice'.

The social and theoretical application of Shakespeare studies seems only to broaden with each particular cultural context it encounters. Such is certainly the message of Paromita Chakravarti and Swati Ganguly's '2002, A Shakespearean Odyssey: Postcolonial Theory and Pedagogy from the Metropolis to the Margins'. If ever there were any doubts about the continued efficacy of overtly theorising about Shakespeare, their examination of the role played by the Bard's works in colonial and postcolonial India is a salutary lesson that theory also still has a major role to play, leading as it does to their proposal for a new and more equitable direction for Subcontinental Shakespearean and literary studies generally. In the United States, supposedly nowhere near the margins of Shakespeare studies, Kay Johnston and Margaret Maurer speak of 'an atmosphere of concern for standards and testing', and make a case in 'Teaching and Risk: Doing and Undoing Shakespeare' for the even wider use of Shakespeare in the classroom as a device for 'provocative disruption' and thus genuine learning as opposed to 'knowing the right answer'.

Czech contributor Pavel Drábek draws upon the European school of 'noetic' criticism in his 'Studying the Art of Provoking' to suggest that making explicit the range of internal responses in the reader/viewer to comparable plays by Shakespeare and his contemporaries leads to the addressing of all manner of fundamental questions about technical choices in and aesthetic appreciation of the dramatic art. At the same time, his chapter reminds us that the study of Shakespeare has for a long time extended well beyond the boundaries of anglophone culture. Finally, John Joughin's 'Pedagogy as Event: a Case Study of *Hamlet* and Hauntology' posits a similar 'new aestheticist' approach, in which students are also 'provoked' into responses based on readings of texts which, like the phantoms and ghosts that often appear in them, 'continue to resist any definitive critical appropriation' and which remain 'beyond our full comprehension'. His chapter also brings us to the brink of a new era of criticism, one that simultaneously embraces all aspects of the modernist and postmodernist modes, yet which may very likely point to something altogether new in terms of our classroom practice and our critical dealings with Shakespeare's work.

Paul Skrebels
Adelaide 2002

Notes

1   This and the other unattributed quotations that follow are taken from the authors' own proposals or chapters, and are hereby acknowledged as their own words.

References

Eaglestone, Robert (2000) *Doing English: A Guide for Literature Students*, London and New York: Routledge.

Easthope, Antony (1991) *Literary into Cultural Studies*, London and New York: Routledge.

Giroux, Henry (1994) 'Doing Cultural Studies: Youth and the Challenge of Pedagogy', *Harvard Educational Review* 64.3: 278–308.

Longhurst, Derek (1982) '"Not for All Time, but for an Age": An Approach to Shakespeare Studies', *Re-Reading English*, ed. Peter Widdowson, London and New York: Methuen, 150–63.

1

Shakespeare, Hegemony and Assessment in New Zealand High Schools

Mark Houlahan

When teachers move from 'teaching' to 'assessing' Shakespeare, whether in English, Media Studies or Drama, their pedagogical aims and purposes tend to become instruments of hegemony. For 'every relationship of hegemony', Gramsci insists, 'is necessarily an educational relationship' (Gramsci 1988: 235). Assessing Shakespeare contributes to raising the 'great mass of the population to a particular cultural and moral level ... a 'cultural-social unity ... on the basis of an equal and common conception of the world' (Gramsci 1988: 348). This sounds grimly abstract, and needs tempering by recalling that hegemony, like history in E.P. Thompson's humane formulation, is 'something which in fact happens and can be shown to have happened in human relationships'; further, he says, those relationships 'must always be embodied in a real people and a real context' (Thompson 1963: 9). The aim of this chapter is thus to examine the specific instance of the intertwining of Shakespeare, assessment and hegemony in the New Zealand education system, where, like much else, 'Shakespeare' is brokered, by means of examination, 'in the interests of dominant socio-cultural and economic groups' (Stoop 1998: 1).

On the morning of November 15, 2001, for example, some thirteen thousand students in New Zealand and throughout the South Pacific experienced this hegemony directly, as they laboured for three hours over their *University Entrance, Bursaries and Scholarships Examination: English* (2001).[1] That occasion was not unique; rather it was typical of the experience of generations of New Zealand students. For the Shakespeare section of the Bursary English exam is in many ways the central location for Shakespeare in the New Zealand High School: its distinct features permit a precise framing of the issues surrounding hegemony and assessment. The exam is taken at the end of year thirteen of pre-tertiary education and functions very much like British 'A' levels or the Australian Higher School Certificate exams. In all three cases, success in the exams determines which tertiary programs students may enter. In New Zealand the exams are national: there are no regional or state variations as in Australia or Great Britain. The Bursary system, moreover, is broad-based and good students usually take five subjects in their examinations. Entry into many professional programs, such as Medicine or Law, is based on an aggregate mark out of 500.[2] The kind of early specialisation the British 'A' level exam encourages is postponed until a later stage of study. This impacts in two key ways on the New Zealand English exam itself: it is taken by a very wide range of students, only some of whom will study further in English and related humanities disciplines; secondly, success in English thus becomes vital for entry into many specialised, non-humanities programs. Partly for these reasons, English is currently the most popular Bursary subject.

All candidates must write on Shakespeare. Twenty per cent of the total mark is allocated to a section on Shakespeare's plays. He is the only compulsory author – the only canonical figure students must tackle, although it is quite common for students to write elsewhere in the exam on classic novelists such as Jane Austen or Thomas Hardy or poets such as John Keats or John Donne. Dealing with Shakespeare thus becomes the central agon for Bursary examinees, a contest students must survive if they are to flourish. In other words, as elsewhere, examining in Shakespeare becomes a classic instrument of hegemony, a crucial way for students to acquire the 'symbolic capital' Western societies require of its citizens to enable them to acquire 'economic capital'. For 'culture' (in this case the cultivation of Shakespeare) 'can have material force' (Harker et al 1990: 207).[3]

Exactly what kind of Shakespeare are these hopeful students thus expected to account for? That issue is the core of this chapter, an analysis of Bursary Shakespeare questions since 1973. This timeframe has been adopted for three main reasons: firstly, a file of the Shakespeare section from 1973–2001 was readily available;[4] secondly, twenty seven years of questions seemed a sufficient length of time to establish clear patterns; thirdly, the period since the mid-1970s has seen marked changes in the focus of Shakespeare scholarship. Most English teachers have taken University English courses in this time: over nearly three decades, it should be possible to see to what extent new ideas have permeated secondary English departments. With these issues in mind I have analysed the questions asked in the exam over this period according to the following topics:

1. What range of work within the Shakespeare canon has been offered to school leavers?
2. What kinds of assessment tasks are being set to establish the Shakespeare 'credentials' of these students?

3. What kinds of questions are students being asked?

The kinds of questions would indicate whether or not 'new approaches' were expected to be understood by the students at secondary level.

1: Canon

Table 1: Bursary Shakespeare Plays: 1973, 1977–2003

Play	Occurrence/29 years	Frequency (%)
Antony & Cleopatra	9	31
As You Like It	12	41.3
Hamlet	2	6.8
2 Henry IV	4	13.7
Henry V	14	41.3
King Lear	17	58.6
Measure for Measure	9	31
Merchant of Venice	5	17.2
Much Ado About Nothing	11	37.9
Othello	15	51.7
Richard III	5	17.2
The Tempest	13	44.8
Twelfth Night	1	3.7

Table 1 shows the answer to the first question. Students answer from a set range of plays each year: the plays are rotated over a three- or four-year cycle. Over this 29-year period, students were asked to account for just thirteen of Shakespeare's 38 plays.[5] The plays offered at year thirteen cover roughly one third of the accepted canon, a rather narrow restriction in focus. The table shows the frequency with which these thirteen have recurred in the Bursary English exams.[6] The list covers tragedies (four), comedies (six) and histories (three); at least one of each has been offered each year, with histories being least popular. In no year was more than one history play offered; and, with only three examples, the range of history plays is the most restricted, with *Henry V* offered far more frequently than *Richard III* or *Henry IV Part II*. This frequency may perhaps partly be attributed to the popularity first of Olivier's and then, in the early 1990s, of Branagh's film of the play.

The Tempest has been the most frequent comedy. Some would perhaps prefer to place this play in the separate, modern, category of 'romance' which has been applied to Shakespeare late plays since the end of the nineteenth century (Massai 2001: 395).[7]

If so, then this would be the only play in that category, for the school canon has found no place for *Cymbeline, Pericles,* or *The Winter's Tale.* Leaving aside *The Tempest, As You Like It* has been the next most frequently set comedy, closely followed by *Much Ado About Nothing, Measure for Measure* and *The Merchant of Venice,* with *Twelfth Night* toiling in the rear with only one appearance in 1973.

Over this period *Othello* and *King Lear* are the big winners, by far the most frequently assessed tragedies, and the two most popular of all the plays, each appearing in just over half the years surveyed. This frequency would also be exacerbated by the fact that, when these plays are on the syllabus, they are chosen by a substantial majority of teachers. For example, in 1999 markers estimated that over eighty per cent of all the answers in the Shakespeare section were on *Othello. King Lear* was rostered back on in 2000, together with *Hamlet.* Seventy-three per cent of all the Shakespeare answers that year were on these two plays, whose centrality to Shakespeare's works was of course enshrined at the beginning of last century in Bradley's *Shakespearean Tragedy* (1904).[8] The dominance of these three tragedies reflects in part, I think, the responsiveness of these lists to canon-formation beyond the classroom. Over the long durée of the twentieth century, their frequency reflects an insistence, since Bradley, that these two plays were the epitome of Shakespearean tragedy. Since tragedy has been held to be the 'first form', by extension these plays become the quintessence of Shakespeare's genius. Teachers persist with these very difficult plays because in part they still wish to expose their classes to the best of what has been felt and thought. On this level, classroom teachers have proven faithful followers of University academics.

A corollary to this dominance is the exclusion of twenty-five out of a possible thirty-eight plays. Some of these exclusions are unsurprising. The lists include no plays that are only partly by Shakespeare. Students are not to be assessed on their knowledge of John Fletcher, for example, so that this excludes the late collaborations *Two Noble Kinsmen* and *Henry VIII.* And if late Shakespeare is off limits, so too is early Shakespeare. The earliest play on the lists is *Richard III*; neither *King John* nor any of the three *Henry VI* plays have been examined. Recent bibliographers would exclude the first two of these on the same grounds as the Fletcher plays, since they may only partly be by Shakespeare. In schools, more likely their absence reflects a reluctance to deal with 'minor' Shakespeare. Perhaps such a reluctance explains also the absence of early comedies such as *Two Gentlemen of Verona, The Comedy of Errors,* or *Loves Labor's Lost,* with the emphasis instead on the 'mature' comedies of around 1600; *Much Ado About Nothing* and *As You Like It* being especial favorites. These last two, of course, would be considered more accessible than the 'stranger' Shakespeare of later plays like *Timon of Athens,* the tragicomic *Troilus and Cressida* or the elaborate early butchery of *Titus Andronicus,* though attitudes to this last play may be changing with the circulation in schools of Julie Taymor's compelling film.

There are some striking exclusions in such a standard list of plays, however: no *Macbeth*, *Romeo and Juliet* or *Midsummer Night's Dream*, plays which resonate well beyond the classroom, and no *Hamlet* until 2000. I suggest that the exclusion of early comedies and problematic later plays represents a form of canonical trickle-down, that is, of 'elitist' ideas about the worth of specific plays filtering down into secondary class-rooms and curricula. The exclusion of more popular Shakespeare plays is probably the reverse flow, a trickle-up, as it were. For although Bursary is the first year where candidates must write on Shakespeare, it is very common for students to be exposed to some Shakespeare earlier in their secondary schooling. Here teachers tend to stick with 'high impact' plays they know will hold their (sometimes-unwilling) students. And, for students who learn better visually than verbally, teachers focus also on texts for which excellent film versions are available. These exclusions can then be explained by a desire not to repeat material in upper years of the school.

2: Assessment & Questions

Table 2: Bursary Shakespeare Questions: 1973, 1977–2002

Question Categories	Occurrence/ 241 questions	Frequency (%)
Theme	7	29.0
Character	117	48.5
Plot	24	9.9
Setting	13	5.3
Genre	2	6.8
Language/Imagery	14	5.8
Quality	1	.4
Reader response	1	.4

In any subject, the nature of the assessment task is always telling; for (content aside) these will show what the teachers of that subject consider to be most important. The questions this section analyses were written by specific examiners, approved by national authorities and marked every year by large teams of markers. In implementing the exam, each individual member of the 'examining body' exercises in specific form the hegemonic demands of a complex system, the educational apparatus of a nation-state. The issue here is therefore not one of blaming (or praising) any one examiner,[9] but rather of seeing how the corporate body comprised of all these functions has shaped a specific kind of Shakespeare. Under that system, English exams since the late 1970s have required a command of the technical skills of close reading. From 1979 onwards (that is, for most of the period surveyed) candidates have been offered a choice of writing either on a general essay question or on a specific passage. In both cases they are expected to demonstrate a synoptic grasp of the play 'as a whole'. In 1979, for example, Lear's 'howl, howl, howl' (V.iii.232) was offered, with the instruction, 'Show how the passage relates to the play as a whole, giving special attention to the sufferings of Lear' – an instruction which, with its emphasis on the subjectivity of the main character and the coherence of the play as a whole, neatly condenses several generations of post-Bradleyan scholarship. The style of questioning, in other words, requires candidates to be New Critics and Formalists. The exams, of course, do not invoke such labels, for it is assumed that high school students will be innocent of such terms.

The protocols of New Criticism seem also to govern the kinds of questions which have been asked over the last twenty years, as displayed in Table 2. The categories used here are necessarily idiosyncratic, and involve qualitative as well as quantitative assessment. This table, as a colleague remarked on reading the first version of this chapter, has been constructed by a non-statistician. The conclusions drawn from the table should thus be read as indicative rather than absolute. Moreover, others examining these questions may think other categories more appropriate. Sometimes, also, questions combine different categories, but for the purpose of this exercise each question has been assigned to one main category.

Character has been by far the dominant preoccupation of these questions (117 questions out of 241). For writing on either *Othello* or *King Lear*, which, as we have seen, candidates have so often been enjoined to do, a prepared character study of a major character would have been sufficient. Those characters, moreover, are assumed to be coherent and explicable, as in this question from 1992:

> Portia speaks boldly about justice in the play, yet treats Shylock harshly. Discuss this and any other ambiguities in the character of Portia.

Since they have to answer five questions in the exam, candidates would have had thirty-five minutes to conduct such a thorough psychoanalytic inquiry.

Theme runs a distant second on this table (70 questions out of 241), with just over a twenty-nine per cent occurrence. Again, these themes are held to cohere throughout the play. In 1981, for example, candidates were asked, for example, to agree (but not disagree) that the theme of 'the conflict between public and private possibilities' was central to *Antony and Cleopatra* as a whole. Historically 1981 might be thought a little early to expect criticism based on deconstructive scepticism and fragmentation to have percolated into secondary classrooms. Yet in 1997 (by which time it might seem quite reasonable to discover some shifts in approach) we find the following:

relate this passage to any THREE important thematic ideas in the play as a whole.

This 'relate ... to the play as a whole' formula was used in 1997 in questions on all five plays in the exam.

The formidable duo of character and theme provide the basis for 77 per cent of all these questions. The remaining 23 per cent are made up of the familiar preoccupations of Leavisite/New Criticism: plot (28), setting (11), imagery/language (12), genre (4) and, coming in below one per cent of all the questions, 'quality' (2). Thus, through their insistence on the coherence and unity of both Shakespeare's plays and their main characters, this generational sample of questions underlines the examinations' contribution to the '"cultural-social" unity [of] a multiplicity of dispersed wills ... welded together ... on the basis of an equal and common conception of the world' (Gramsci 1988: 348). Shakespeare, it is assumed, continues to hold the mirror up to our natures and our societies.

3: Brave New World?

What then of the many new readings of Shakespeare the past generation of critics have produced, lucidly described in the recent *Cambridge Companion to Shakespeare* (de Grazia and Wells, 2001)? What of queer, feminist and post-colonial Shakespeare? What of Shakespeare here down-under, and elsewhere? What of the psychoanalysts' Shakespeare or the New Historicist Shakespeare? What of Shakespeare in (live) performance or Shakespeare on screen? What of Shakespeare in cultural history?

The exams, for the most part, remain innocent of such matters. Only eight of the 241 questions (3%) seem to gesture towards such new approaches, such as questions on the female characters in *Richard III* ('discuss the roles of women in *Richard III*', as the 2001 exam put it) and *Henry V*; on the relationship between Prospero and Caliban in *The Tempest*; and on the issue of race, as in the 1998 invitation to 'discuss some of the ways in which race contributes to the tragedy of Othello'. The resistance to such readings – which, as Vaughan's (1994) and Pechter's (1999) studies have shown, have dominated *Othello* scholarship over the last twenty years – is eloquently suggested by the following comment sent to the Chief Marker by a concerned teacher:

> Of course race is an issue but it is not a vital enough issue to allow students to write essays of depth in content, thought, and argument. In other words, to do themselves justice. One wonders why the venerable BBC video cast Othello as European.[10]

Here a current approach is emphatically closed down; the rhetoric used here, 'vital', 'depth', and 'venerable', opens out instead into a Leavisite past.

Some of the questions which look current (but turn out not to be) perform similar manoeuvres. For example, the 1999 exam offered this question, which raised the interesting issue of local performance:

> This year a Wellington production of *Much Ado About Nothing* set the play just after World War I: Benedick, Don Pedro and the other soldiers played as New Zealand soldiers returning from battlefields of Europe. What do war and soldiers have to do with the social world of Messina we see in the play?

In Table 2 this was ranked as a question about setting (though it could also be ranked as a question about theme). Note the way the question raises issues both of 'performance' Shakespeare and 'New Zealand' Shakespeare, only to turn away from them to raise its 'real' question. Film scholars would be equally disappointed by this question from 1994:

> *Henry V* has been produced on stage and film as an experience of nationalistic pride (as it as by Laurence Olivier), and as an indictment of war (as it was by Kenneth Branagh). Which, in your view, is the more satisfactory reading of the play?

Here candidates are asked to be aware of these two famous films, key moments in the recent performance history of the play. But they are not asked to discuss the films. Rather their proper business is held to be the 'satisfactory reading of the play'. And the words of the play itself, as in all these questions, is held to be grounds sufficient for producing such a reading.

English teaching in New Zealand schools has been governed since 1994 by the *English in the New Zealand Curriculum* document. This requires that students, in their final years at secondary school, be able to 'interpret, evaluate and produce written texts … identifying … their language and literary qualities and relating them to personal, social, cultural, political and historical contexts' (*English* 1994: 88). As a response to this statutory requirement, the Bursary Shakespeare questions address the first two (language and 'literary' qualities) and ignore the final five, turning aside both the demands of the High School curriculum and the contemporary currents of Shakespeare scholarship. The questions are created in a backwater, a timewarp. A minority of the students who write the Bursary exam will read Shakespeare in universities, and will discover (hopefully) many new Shakespeares in lectures and tutorials, in essays and in libraries, on screen and on stage. Most will never again read a Shakespeare play: *their* Shakespeare inevitably will retain this conservative, non-dramatic, non-cinematic cast.

Beyond the classroom there are signs of lively local, theatrical interventions into Shakespeare, from the high farce of Jean Betts' burlesques of *A Midsummer Night's Dream* (*Revenge of the Amazons*, 1983) and *Hamlet* (*Ophelia Thinks Harder*, 1993) through the interracial verve of Pacific Underground's Samoan/Maori *Romeo and Tusi* (2000) to the 2002 release of a feature film in Maori of *The Merchant of Venice*. From 2004 a new *National Certificate of Educational Achievement* will replace the current Bursary system. Under this system, students will be assessed both internally and by external, national examination. School leavers will achieve 'level three' qualifications, and be ranked according to their ability in eight strands of each subject. In theory, they acquire a more detailed profile of their skills, through which employers understand better who – or what – they are hiring. And yet, when much else changes, Shakespeare survives. The declared draft standard for *NCEA Level Three English* requires students to 'respond critically to Shakespearean drama', awarding the highest standards of 'excellence' to students whose work integrates 'supporting evidence' and 'demonstrates sustained insight'. As in the current system, five plays a year will be gazetted as the official 'canon' to be covered. To judge from preliminary seminars preparing teachers for this new system, the assessment tasks will be markedly similar to the system now in place.

Canons, of taste or lists of texts, always imply choices. Some texts are chosen, some not; some lines of inquiry are encouraged, some frowned upon. The conservatism of the system this chapter describes looks likely to last well into the new century, with the effective Shakespeare canon in New Zealand High Schools coalescing around the great tragedies Bradley made central. Correspondingly, the two-thirds of the canon rendered invisible by the recently examined 'canon' of plays look likely to remain 'minor' Shakespeare, unread by most secondary students and teachers. As well, it seems that lines of inquiry into those plays which are read will also change but slowly. Teachers conscientiously seek to interpret the demands of the assessment mechanism, guiding students to respond to old-fashioned questions about theme and character. To do otherwise will leave them open to charges of neglecting their professional duties. No single teacher could change such a system, for, short of 'revolution', change is liable to be incremental and slow, and the specific form of hegemony I have described will be hard to shift. But at the very least teachers can be aware of the implications of such (apparently) innocent gestures as selecting the play a class is to study, or isolating the 'themes' and 'characters' to be revised: essays on same due next Friday.

Notes

1   This is the generic title for the exam. For convenience, I will not cite the full title throughout this chapter. Rather, when citing questions, I will simply give the year in which each question appeared.

2   Less competitive programs, such as first year arts and social science programs, require 'C' grades (forty-five per cent or higher) in only three subjects. Thus some students fill out their program with elective, less 'academic' options.

3   Here Harker, Mahar and Wilkes are summarising arguments most forcefully put by the late Pierre Bourdieu.

4   Ralph Crane, Linda Keith, Jeanine and Richard Grahame provided these essential resources. The sample thus relies on their holdings. Compiling statistics for twenty nine years of examination scripts seemed enough to establish indicative trends.

5   These figures are taken from the Oxford Shakespeare's report of the canon, thus including the collaborations *Two Noble Kinsmen* and *Henry VIII*, but excluding the most recent addition of *Edward III* to the *Riverside Shakespeare* and the New Cambridge series.

6   These frequencies include 2002 and 2003 because, although the November exams for these are not available at the time of writing, the roster of plays has already been circulated.

7   Categorising *The Tempest* as 'comedy', in contrast, derives from the 1623 *First Folio* of Shakespeare's plays, from which the genre categories 'histories' and 'tragedies' are derived.

8   These figures are taken from the New Zealand Qualifications Authority (NZQA) *Marking Schedule and Examination Commentary* (1999) p. 1; and for 2000, from NZQA's memo on 'Language topics and Shakespeare plays for 2002 and 2003' of 26 January 2001.

9   Typically there has been a change of chief examiner every three or four years over this period. The task of marking the exam has been rotated around major New Zealand cities.

10 Communication sent to NZQA, who administer the exam, in November 1998, and provided to me by Ralph Crane, chief examiner of that year. I print this comment anonymously, as indicative of certain attitudes. In the collective memory of teachers and those who took that exam, the question continues to be controversial.

References

Bradley, A.C. (1964) *Shakespearian Tragedy*, London: Macmillan.

de Grazia, M. and Wells, S. (2001) (eds) *Cambridge Companion to Shakespeare Studies*, Cambridge: Cambridge University Press.

Draft Achievement Standard: English 3.3: Respond critically to Shakespearian drama (2000) Wellington: Crown.

English in the New Zealand Curriculum (1994) Wellington, New Zealand: Learning Media.

Gramsci, A. (1988) *An Antonio Gramsci Reader: Selected Writings, 1916–1935*, trans. Hoare, Q. and Novell-Smith, G. ed. Forgacs, D. New York: Schocken Books.

Harker, R., Mahar, C. and Wilkes, C. (1990) (eds) *An Introduction to the Work of Pierre Bourdieu*, London: MacMillan.

Houlahan, M. (2000) 'The Return of the King? Reading the Bard and Roland Barthes,' *English in Aotearoa* 40 (May 2000): 24–26.

Massai, S. (2001) 'Romance' in Dobson, M. and Wells, S. (eds) *The Oxford Companion to Shakespeare*, Oxford: Oxford University Press, 395.

Pechter, Edward (1999) *Othello and Interpretive Traditions*, Iowa City: Iowa University Press.

Shakespeare, William (1994) *The Complete Works*, (eds) Wells S. and Taylor, G. Oxford: Oxford University Press.

Sinfield, A. (1985) 'Give an account of Shakespeare and Education, showing why you think they are effective and what you have appreciated about them. Support your comments with precise references' in Dollimore, J. and Sinfield, A. (eds) *Political Shakespeare: New Essays on Cultural Materialism*, Ithaca:Cornell University Press, 134–158.

Stoop, Graham Charles (1998) *The Management of Knowledge: Text, Context, and the New Zealand English Curriculum*, PhD thesis, University of Canterbury, Christchurch, New Zealand.

Thompson, E.P. (1963) *The Making of the English Working Class*, London: Victor Gollancz.

Vaughan, Virginia Mason (1994) *Othello: A Contextual History*, Cambridge: Cambridge University Press.

2

Exposing Shakespeare

INTRODUCING ENGLISH STUDIES AT UNIVERSITY

Catherine Silverstone

Since 1988 first-year students majoring in English at the University of Sussex (UK) have been required to take a course in their first term entitled 'Historical Approaches to Shakespeare' (HATS). The rubric, developed by the English Subject Group (ESG), states that:

> [t]he course will introduce students to the range of critical approaches to literature, their changing history and contexts, and the different forms of reading which they produce. It will do this by studying the history of the reading of *Shakespeare* in relation to four or more works by *Shakespeare*, the author, who, more than any other, has over a long period been the focus of key intellectual debates constituting and transforming the criticism of English literature and the discipline of English studies. (*Index of Undergraduate Courses 1999–2000*: 131)

Using this rubric, tutors, who can be either a member of faculty or a postgraduate such as myself, are invited to design their own ten-week course and accompanying assessment.[1] In conjunction with attending a lecture series which provides a historical overview of developments in Shakespeare criticism, from the Restoration to queer Shakespeare, students meet with their tutor and approximately 14 other students for a two-hour seminar once a week.

Ostensibly, the course looks straightforward: criticism of Shakespeare will be used to chart the history of English studies. A logical choice in terms of the battery of criticism that Shakespeare has engendered over the last 400 years, the use of Shakespeare, however, effectively locates him at the centre of the canon of English studies; a canon which much recent criticism has sought to disrupt. Simultaneously, the course displaces Shakespeare, overwriting him with scholarship as it works to give literary theory and criticism a history. In this way it offers a neat pedagogical gloss on an English department which has a reputation for critical theory and the analysis of Shakespeare as a cultural phenomenon (see for example Dollimore and Sinfield 1994). Drawing on my experiences of teaching and redesigning the course, this chapter will engage with issues of pedagogical practice and canonicity. In so doing I aim to provide a model for effectively introducing first-year students to both English studies and Shakespeare in a way which also equips them with a range of 'transferable' academic skills.

Students studying Shakespeare at a British university are rarely encountering his texts for the first time. The majority of my students had read at least one Shakespeare play in the course of their school studies in English. Imbued with the legacy of A. C. Bradley and F. R. Leavis, their analysis, for the most part, was focussed on the 'close reading' a play, usually over a period of several weeks, with much attention given to plot, theme, character and imagery (Sinfield 1994: 158–81). In addition my students were largely innocent of recent critical approaches, a phenomenon which, as Mark Houlahan's incisive commentary on the Bursary English exam in New Zealand demonstrates,[2] is not isolated to the British secondary school context. At the beginning of the course the students tended to be resistant to reading literary criticism, preferring instead to discuss character motivation and emotions. Perhaps the salient feature, however, of their attitudes toward Shakespeare is that he is *good*, or as one student put it, there was '[m]uch "bardolatry"' in the secondary school classroom. The course I designed thus aimed at exposing these practices and ideas as cultural constructions and attempted to explore some of the assumptions that inform different methods of reading and analysis. I thus sought to show, for example, that character analysis is *one* method of reading, which in the case of Bradley depends on a humanist understanding of the subject and a desire to treat literary characters as 'real' people. By tackling (perhaps naively) such a broad sweep of criticism I also aimed to look at the way in which Shakespeare has been instituted as a cultural icon. In short, by encouraging my students to be critical and questioning readers I wanted to widen the scope of their previous study of Shakespeare, making them aware that literary criticism exists in many forms and that each form, like Shakespeare's plays, is a product of the historical moment of its production.

After an introductory session students read one Shakespeare play and two or three critical articles a week, with each article broadly representative of a different approach. Beginning with *Othello* students sampled a range of pre-twentieth century analyses including Samuel Johnson's (1968) *Preface* and Thomas Rymer's (1974) vitriolic attack on the play. Teaching *Othello* over a two-week period, partially in an effort to gradually increase their reading speeds, I asked the students to read critical overview articles by Harry Levin (1986) and John Drakakis (1985) and to construct a chronology of some of the major developments in criticism. Rather than proposing a fixed linear chronology, I intended this exercise to provide the students with a broad picture of some of the major developments in English studies. Drakakis's introduction to *Alternative Shakespeares* (1985) also performed a double function of challenging essentialist views about humanity and Shakespeare which tend to be dominant in the secondary school classroom; instead he suggests that Shakespeare's texts are remade to suit different ideological projects at different times.

Although the students found these articles difficult, these authors did present Shakespeare and English studies as a many-faceted phenomenon; one which the following seminars sought to illustrate by exposing the students to various critical movements of the twentieth century, including character analysis, cultural materialism, feminism, formalism, new criticism, new historicism, performance studies, postcolonialism and queer studies. Thus, in preparation for a seminar on *Twelfth Night*, students read Stephen Greenblatt's article 'Fiction and Friction' (1988), and Valerie Traub's (1992) analysis of the homoerotics in *Twelfth Night* and *As You Like It* as a way of introducing ideas about new historicism and queer studies. With such an extensive critical survey students were not expected to be cognisant of the nuances of each movement. Rather I wanted them to gain an awareness of the variety which exists in English studies and an appreciation of some of the major critical developments, especially in the twentieth century.

For students used to reading a play over a long period of time, and unused to reading much criticism at all, the sheer volume of reading poses an immediate challenge to enable students to read quickly and critically. My solution to this problem was threefold. First, using brainstorming activities, initially in groups and then as a class, we talked about skills for reading articles and plays which were consolidated with practical examples and a handout on 'reading guidelines'. By way of a follow-up activity I often started subsequent seminars by asking the students to comment on an article's style, structure, terms they didn't understand and how they went about dealing with any problems. In these discussions we worked through practical guidelines for making reading more productive, such as consulting a dictionary or a glossary of literary terms and outlining methods for locating an article's key points.

Second, each week I provided the students with a list of questions to consider while they read the articles. In order to counteract students' sometimes feeling 'lost' as they read, I included these 'guiding' questions as an addition to the way I had previously taught the course. These questions flagged the topics for each seminar. Thus for the class on feminism students were asked to identify what Kathleen McLuskie (1994) focuses on in her reading of *Measure for Measure* and then invited to consider what they would focus on if they were asked to write a feminist analysis of the play. Here the students were required to both analyse what a critic has argued and develop their own ideas on the topic. At the risk of closing down some avenues of discussion, the questions did help prevent students from 'drifting' and encouraged an attentive, focused reading of the texts. This in turn provided the basis for class discussion on the articles and the wider issues they raised.

Third, for the first four weeks of term students were asked to write 300-word journal entries on one of the articles assigned for each week. This ensured that they were reading, thinking and writing early in the course. Grading the journals at fortnightly intervals also enabled me to offer early feedback on written work and to check their understanding of the material. While some students were a little unclear as to what was expected of a journal entry, which suggests that my task writing may require some clarification, I generally found that this exercise, especially in conjunction with the guiding questions, worked well. Indeed, one student reported that 'the journal entries and the questions we were asked to think about [were] very helpful in developing ... critical reading and writing skills'. Others commented that the journals 'were useful to focus what ... [they] had learned in the reading' and helped them 'concentrate on ... [the] reading'. Several also claimed that the journal was useful preparation, in terms of writing practice and content, for the final essay.

The final essay asked students to consider the issues the course raises and provided opportunities for them to enhance their skills in structuring an argument and writing clearly. As such they had the choice of developing and explaining their own reading practice. Thus several students wrote essays about factors a critic might want to consider when reading gender and sexuality in the early modern period. Other essay topics asked students to take a stand on a proposition, such as whether the meaning of a Shakespeare play is consistent and unchanging through time. Overall the students responded well to what were very wide ranging essay questions. As well as finding the topics challenging and relatively difficult, survey responses suggest that the essay made the students think critically. One student wrote: the '[e]ssay was a really good experience (!) because it showed me how much I had learned and how I actually had my own ideas'; another reported that the essay was enjoyable 'because I was able to develop a fuller argument, really drawing aspects of the course together'. Dissatisfaction with the experience included problems with the location of the deadline, a request for a longer word limit and difficulty with the breadth of the questions, all of which invite consideration when I redesign the course. Interestingly, several admitted, sometimes rather shyly, that they would have liked another essay in addition to the journal entries and final paper. I am inclined to agree as there was probably too great an interval between the last journal entry and the essay. In comparison to the previous year, where I only set two pieces of written work, I feel that small, continuous writing tasks offer the best opportunity for first year students to develop their writing skills and gain confidence working in a university environment.

While writing tasks accounted for 70 per cent of the final grade, the remaining 30 per cent was reserved for an oral presentation, enabling students to gain skills in verbal communication. I offered three presentation options which could be undertaken individually or in a group. Students could either: a) give a short talk on some aspect of the reading which they found interesting; b) devise a role play which related to that week's texts; or c) act out a short section from that week's play. Unlike the other tasks which were directly focused on literary criticism, the presentation options, especially b) and c), gave students space to directly address the play texts, an absence many of them had found disappointing when they began the course. The results were generally very impressive. One pair presented a role-play between Caliban and a psychoanalyst. They had collected a range of visual representations of Caliban and as each picture was presented on the overhead projector their presentation explored the way Caliban has been represented, thus raising questions about cultural difference, visual representation and colonialism. Covering similar issues, another student produced a Caliban 'performance piece', creating a pastiche monologue from the play, his own thoughts and criticism. Another group presented the gender and sexuality confusions in the 'camp' style of a Graham Norton chat show complete with bras for boys and false moustaches for girls, opening up a discussion on gender and sexual identity difference. Students who opted to give a more 'conventional' talk made good use of video, produced handouts to aid class understanding and devised questions to provoke discussion. The difference in the presentation quality between the first and second years I taught the course was dramatic. In large part I think this was a result of having made my expectations much clearer in my second year of teaching the course.

As well as teaching through assessment activities the seminar environment provided a weekly forum for learning. Because much emphasis is placed on student discussion, I find that it is imperative that students feel relaxed and comfortable in the classroom and that clear expectations are established at the beginning of the course as to what is required of the students and myself. In the utopian world of possibilities provided by the first class we all undertook to be well prepared, organised and willing to participate. I also worked to create a positive, relaxed and energetic learning space where all students felt that their opinions were valued. In conjunction with a mix of media such as video, transparencies and board-work, I also used a variety of learning styles including small group work, particularly at the beginning of term. This format allows quieter students to participate early in the course and works to prevent, not always successfully, dominant students from taking control. While I find the seminar format to be a particularly rich method of teaching, especially since it avoids the generally passive intake of information which the lecture room promotes, students sometimes struggle with processing large volumes of information without 'concrete' notes. Indeed one student felt that they were '[l]eft to be too independent too early'. One way in which I plan to combat this problem is by providing short handouts covering the key points for each week.

So, in the process of helping students to read and think more critically and gain an awareness of shifts in Shakespeare and English studies, what was the course teaching them about Shakespeare and canonicity? That is, how might one include debates about canonicity within a course expressly concerned with Shakespeare and criticism? One way I went about raising ideas about canonicity was by challenging the internal Shakespeare canon by including a seminar on *Titus Andronicus*. *Titus* has a long history of being vilified as an inferior Shakespeare play, with T. S. Eliot famously declaring that *Titus* was 'one of the stupidest and most uninspired plays ever written' (1951: 82). To counteract the evident 'embarrassment' at having to ascribe such a play to Shakespeare, historically critics have dismissed it as a piece of juvenilia or in more extreme cases claim that Shakespeare did not write the play at all. It is hardly a popular choice for school exam study and none of my students had read the play before the course. After reading the play and watching Julie Taymor's 1999 film, *Titus*, many of my students confessed to being shocked by the ultra-violence of the dismemberment of hands, heads and tongues and the rape of Lavinia. By including this play I aimed to explore something of the way the Shakespeare canon has been constructed and raise an awareness of the variety within the canon. In future I would also like to experiment with including a narrative poem to further widen the students' perception of Shakespeare and to expose them to other literary genres of the early modern period.[3]

As well as internally challenging the canon, I chose several critical articles that placed the plays within the context of other early modern texts. Most notably these included Emily C. Bartels's article on *Othello* (1990) which reads the issue of race in the play alongside *Titus Andronicus*, Richard Hakluyt's *Principal Navigations* and Leo Africanus's *A Geographical Historie of Africa*; and Greenblatt's 'Fiction and Friction' (1988) which, as an exemplar of New Historicism, reads *Twelfth Night* in conjunction with anecdotes about early modern cross-dressing and medical tracts. In addition to providing examples of current reading practices and opening up discussions about recent critical concerns such as race, gender and sexuality, my intention of including articles such as these was to disrupt the idea that Shakespeare exists in a literary and cultural vacuum. This strategy was fairly successful with students mostly reporting that it was important to study Shakespeare alongside other early modern authors as 'it puts him in context', 'stops Shakespeare from being isolated' and helps 'put Shakespeare in perspective'. Ideally, then, a course such as this should include, as is the practice in New Historicist and Cultural Materialist criticism, some texts by other early modern writers to help ground the Shakespeare canon more firmly as the product of a particular time and culture.

My final strategy for opening up questions of canon formation was implemented as part of a seminar on *The Tempest*. For this class students read the play, Paul Brown's article on *The Tempest* (1994) and discourses of colonialism and Rob Nixon's discussion of a series of African and Caribbean appropriations of *The Tempest* (1987). Nixon's article in particular, which refers to how *The Tempest* has been reworked as a text of liberation from colonial rule, provided scope for a discussion on the way Shakespeare has been used as a colonising tool. It also encouraged a discussion on the way in which the English canon might be negotiated, especially by groups it tends to elide. As with expanding the Shakespeare and early modern canons, the course might benefit from the inclusion of a short text which reworks Shakespeare in order to illustrate the idea of appropriation in more detail.[4]

Within the frame of a course such as this it is, therefore, possible to interrogate the canonical position of Shakespeare in the process of introducing English studies. Indeed several students thought we should study Shakespeare to help students understand how he has become 'establishment' and another claimed the course had 'given me a ... broader picture of studying English. ... [and] opened my eyes to the wider historical and cultural picture'. However, even after a term of reading criticism which frequently disrupts an essentialist, bardolotrous Shakespeare, he still survives, to some extent, as the great genius of English literature, unchallenged at the heart of the canon. Indeed one student wrote that 'a law should be made to make everyone study Shakespeare. It is so fantastic'; another proclaimed, 'it's a universal tradition and he is one of the greatest master[s] of literature'. Perhaps finally the only way to disrupt the Shakespeare-centric view of literary studies which the course unavoidably proposes, even as it seeks to displace it, is to stop teaching so much Shakespeare (criticism).

In many ways, then, I attempted to design a course that was less about Shakespeare and more about developing skills in orally presenting, reading, writing, thinking critically and in acquiring an understanding about English studies. Students reported learning 'to adopt a more critical approach', gaining an awareness of 'the different literary movements' and reading quickly. I suggest that to effectively teach this kind of course involves addressing historical and current approaches to literature, being aware of the variety of ways in which students learn, responding to student feedback and continually assessing one's own critical ideas and pedagogical practice. For postgraduate tutors, who are often vulnerably employed on temporary contracts and isolated with respect to a peer group and access to facilities, this also means taking advantage of all training opportunities that an institution might provide and actively seeking a teaching mentor.[5] Influenced by extraordinary colleagues, my own teaching practices and the course I designed aimed to equip students with the skills to enter into debates about Shakespeare, with both a historical awareness of the practice of literary criticism and an appreciation of the multiple ways in which the discipline of English studies operates at the beginning of the new millennium.[6]

The ESG at Sussex has recently undertaken a curriculum review and Shakespeare will cease to be so dominant in first-year course offerings. As of 2003 HATS will no longer continue to be taught. Instead it will be replaced with a general introductory course which looks at a range of texts from different periods. This does not remove the question of canon formation but creates a broader base from which to explore these issues than that provided by HATS. Such a course should be able to introduce students not only to the diversity of English studies but also gesture to the enormous variety of literatures in English. As students still tend to arrive at university largely unaware of the theory and history of English studies, I would suggest that the pedagogical work of HATS is not yet done. However, a format where Shakespeare plays one part among many might do this work more effectively. Given the shock to the intellectual system HATS provides, encapsulated by a student who felt that the rug had been pulled out from under their collective feet with respect to English studies, perhaps the biggest lesson it can offer to teachers at schools and universities is that these institutions could, even within the confines of conservative school examination syllabi, benefit from working together more closely. In this way students might be given the opportunity to better understand English studies as it operates today throughout their educational careers.

Notes

1   There is no final exam and the course does not count toward the class of a student's degree. However, students do need to pass the course in order to be admitted to second year courses.

2   See Chapter 1 in the present collection, Mark Houlahan's 'Shakespeare, Hegemony and Assessment in New Zealand Schools'.

3   See Chapter 8, Mary J. Metzger's 'To "See Feelingly": Reading Shakespeare's *The Rape of Lucrece*', for just such a project.

4   See Chapter 6, Paul Skrebels' 'Shakespeare Reworked: Textual Intervention Strategies in a University Writing Classroom'.

5   The Chair of the ESG runs a mentoring scheme and the University of Sussex offers a postgraduate tutors' training course under the auspices of the Staff Development Unit.

6   My thanks are due to: Margaret Healy, Mark Houlahan, Kirstine Moffat and Dorothy Spiller whose own teaching practices inspire me to constantly strive to improve my own. I would also like to offer many thanks to my students at the University of Sussex in 2000 and 2001, especially those who so graciously completed my seemingly endless questionnaire. All quotations from students are taken from two anonymous teaching questionnaires completed by 21 students on 14 December 2001 at the University of Sussex. Spelling has been corrected. All italics occur in the original texts.

References

Bartels, E.C. (1990) 'Making More of the Moor: Aaron, Othello, and Renaissance Refashionings of Race' *Shakespeare Quarterly* 41.4: 433–54.

Bradley, A.C. (1992) *Shakespearean Tragedy*, 3rd ed, Houndmills: Macmillan.

Brown, P. (1994) '"This thing of darkness I acknowledge mine": *The Tempest* and the Discourse of Colonialism', Dollimore and Sinfield, 48–71.

Dollimore, J. and Sinfield, A. (eds) (1994) *Political Shakespeare: Essays in Cultural Materialism*, 2nd ed, Manchester: Manchester University Press.

Drakakis, J. (1985) 'Introduction', Drakakis J. (ed) *Alternative Shakespeares*, London: Routledge, 1–25.

Eliot, T.S. (1951) 'Seneca in Elizabethan Translation', *Selected Essays 1917–1932*, 3rd ed, London: Faber and Faber, 65–105.

Greenblatt, S. (1988) 'Friction and Fiction', *Shakespearean Negotiations: The Circulation of Social Energy in Renaissance England*, Berkeley: University of California Press, 66–93.

Index of Undergraduate Courses 1999–2000 (1999) Brighton: University of Sussex Printing Unit.

Johnson, S. (1968) *Preface to Shakespeare*, Sherbo, A. (ed) *Johnson on Shakespeare*, Vol. 1, New Haven: Yale University Press, 59–92.

Leavis, F.R. (1952) *The Common Pursuit*, London: Chatto and Windus.

Levin, H. (1986) 'Critical Approaches to Shakespeare 1660–1904', Wells, S. (ed) *Cambridge Companion to Shakespeare Studies*, Cambridge: Cambridge University Press, 1986, 213–29.

McLuskie, K. (1994) 'The Patriarchal Bard: Feminist Criticism and Shakespeare: *King Lear* and *Measure for Measure*', Dollimore and Sinfield, 88–108.

Nixon, R. (1987) 'Caribbean and African Appropriations of *The Tempest*' *Critical Inquiry* 13: 557–78.

Rymer, T. (1974) *A Short View of Tragedy*, Vickers, B. (ed) *Shakespeare: The Critical Heritage*, Vol. 2, London: Routledge, 25–54.

Sinfield, A. (1994) 'Give an account of Shakespeare and education, showing why you think they are effective and what you have appreciated about them. Support your comments with precise references', Dollimore and Sinfield, 158–81.

Titus (motion picture) (1999), Clear Blue Sky Productions, directed by Julie Taymor, starring Anthony Hopkins and Jessica Lange.

Traub, V. (1992) *Desire and Anxiety: Circulations of Sexuality in Shakespearian Drama*, London: Routledge, 117–44.

3

An Approach to
Teaching Shakespeare

KING LEAR AND THE NEW SENIOR

ENGLISH SYLLABUS IN

NEW SOUTH WALES

Derek Peat

A visitor inquired of me recently, 'What do you do with a play of Shakespeare?' 'Act it,' I replied. 'What else can you do with a play?' What the old-fashioned pedant could do to a play of Shakespeare is too well known to bear relation, but, incredible though it may seem, it is still rare to find acting the principal means of dealing with plays in school. (Cook 1917: 194–95)

Caldwell Cook, an English schoolteacher, made that comment over eighty years ago. In 1980 I quoted it in an interview with J.L. Styan on teaching Shakespeare (Peat 1980: 142), because it seemed to me equally true of the situation I had been experiencing in the late seventies.

I should admit at the start that I had long believed that Shakespeare did need protecting – from the education system! This was why, with a group of actors, I presented workshops on the Shakespeare text set for the final exam in English in NSW, the Higher School Certificate (HSC). I would begin by pointing out to the students that Shakespeare didn't write their particular play for the HSC and that he probably would have been somewhat bemused by what they were doing – reading his play to answer exam questions about it. If they were reading it to see if they wished to perform it, he would have understood, but performance was far from most students' minds. We then explored the play by performing various scenes not one way, but multiple ways, constantly involving the audience in an ongoing discussion about what was happening. The idea was to see what the play was capable of, what effects could be created, how it could be made to live. It was also an attempt to protect the play from the predatory effect of exams and the dead hand of a school system that paid little attention to the fact that plays are intended for performance.

In those days I was teaching at a University and now I teach in a High School. And besides, this was in the days of the old syllabus and that particular wench is dead. In the year 2000, a new Senior English Syllabus was introduced in NSW. The syllabus planners wanted to do a great many things and in the process make English more relevant to the lives of today's students. The idea of 'text' in the old course had been traditional, but now it was expanded to embrace modern text types such as film, television, CD-ROM and the Internet. 'Text' itself was now balanced by the idea of 'context' and the course tended to focus on ideas, using multiple texts to explore these rather than a single text. The new syllabus thus took into account the changes in thinking about the subject itself brought about by 'theory', and also sought to secure a better balance between having the students 'responding' to texts and 'composing' them. Along with all this went a series of political imperatives. Any government introducing changes to the ways English is taught needs to take with it an electorate suspicious of 'trendy' new approaches and already worried by educational standards (the popular misconception being that English and 'literacy' go hand-in-hand). The introduction of so much that was new was made more palatable by a simultaneous emphasis on the importance of classic texts and as usual Shakespeare was the major representative. Traditionalist teachers and parents were reassured as the opportunities to study the plays expanded.

So with this new syllabus does Shakespeare still need saving? I suspect the answer remains 'Yes' because in the English course, in Cook's words, 'It is still rare to find acting the principal means of dealing with plays in school' (Cook 1917: 195).

I

I'm concerned here with the module 'Critical Study of Texts' which is part of 'Advanced English', a course taken by the top third of the candidates. In some ways the most traditional part of the new syllabus, even here the course description indicates that things have changed:

> This module requires students to explore and evaluate a specific text and its reception in a range of contexts. It develops students' understandings of questions of textual integrity. (Board of Studies of NSW 1999: 19)

When we come to the description of what students will do with the play we find this:

> Students who choose the Shakespeare play explore its literary qualities and the ways in which different readings are possible and imply different values that may be realised through different productions. (Board of Studies of NSW 1999: 19)

This all remains pretty general, but the sample exam distributed to schools brings the expectations into clearer focus (in the light of my comments above, I'm aware of the irony that teachers learn about what the course requires from considering a sample exam question):

'Every new reading of *King Lear* implies a reconsideration of the ways in which audiences value the play and respond to it.'

Discuss this view with reference to TWO scenes from the play and how these scenes impact on the play as a whole. (Board of Studies of NSW 2000: 4)[1]

In some ways this is business as usual; there is a greater emphasis on performance ('the ways in which audiences … respond'), but even the old syllabus had nodded in the direction of a play being a text for performance even though many teachers simply ignored this. The newness is in the additional emphasis ('every new reading … implies a reconsideration of the ways in which audiences value …'), which requires students to have knowledge of the various contexts in which such transmissions take place.

So far, so good, but how can this translate into classroom activity? Comments made to me by both students and teachers from a number of schools suggest that there has been a good deal of emphasis on the kind of approach that considers a 'postmodern interpretation', a 'feminist interpretation', a 'historicist interpretation' and so on. It seems to me to rework Caldwell Cook's comment that we are in danger of subjecting the students to 'what the new-fashioned pedant could do to a play of Shakespeare.'

My own teaching of Shakespeare has always been informed by the belief that students learn best by working with the text through performance. If this is done under something approximating 'original' performance conditions, it can lead quite naturally into an exploration of performances through time and of the ways in which audiences may value and respond.

So how do we begin? I know some colleagues who believe that it is essential to start with an actual performance, usually on video, so that students get the opportunity to 'see' the play before they begin any kind of exploration, even a reading. I think this may actually close off, rather than open up, performance possibilities (and it has the added problem that it already requires a complex understanding of the contexts of the particular performance), so I work exactly the other way around.

Before we begin any work on *King Lear* I ask the students to do something remarkably old-fashioned: to read it right through (of course there's a great difference between my asking for this and it happening!) and also to keep a 'Lear Log'. In their

Log they record anything they choose – problems, difficulties of understanding, words or lines that catch their attention, and particularly their personal responses to what is happening.

I emphasise that their first reading could reveal valuable insights, because it places them in the position of an audience experiencing the play for the first time – and a single performance is the way most audiences experience any play. If, for example, they wonder what will happen next (a natural thing for any audience to do), and if they find that what they expected is contradicted by the action, they are having a direct response to the play. Similarly, if they aren't sure what is happening and why, once again this should be clearly noted, because it could be that Shakespeare was creating such confusion to secure a particular dramatic effect. I ask them to update their Logs as we study the play, so they can check their early impressions against their later thoughts.[2]

My work in the classroom involves read-throughs and workshop performances so the students can make a scene their own before they see how others have interpreted it. After such work we might go on to look at a couple of video performances and analyse their effects. Working this way has the advantage of enabling students to understand the basis of the decisions that have been taken in actual performances, because they themselves have been through this decision-making process.

I should emphasise that we are not in a drama class here – the point is not to develop a polished performance, but rather to explore the play itself through performance. To do this well, everyone in the classroom needs to be involved in a workshop lesson. It won't work if a few individuals are the 'actors' and the rest just watch. Through constantly changing roles, as many students as possible should get the opportunity to be involved as both actors and audience members, that is, in both creating and perceiving effects and in both giving and receiving feedback. Obviously, it takes some time for a teacher to gain the trust of the students and for the students themselves to develop the confidence to risk looking foolish before their peers.

The following section is a description of work done on *King Lear* in one fifty minute period, with a Year Twelve class who had also had me as their teacher the previous year, when we had worked on another Shakespeare play.

II

The scene we worked on, Act V scene ii, is conveniently short:

> *Alarum within. Enter with drum and colours*
> LEAR, CORDELIA and Soldiers, *over the stage and exeunt.*
>
> *Enter* EDGAR, *dressed like a peasant, and* GLOUCESTER.

EDGAR

    Here, father, take the shadow of this tree

    For your good host; pray that the right may thrive.

    If ever I return to you again

    I'll bring you comfort.

GLOUCESTER

    Grace go with you, sir.

                         Exit. [Edgar]

Alarum and retreat within. Enter EDGAR.

EDGAR

    Away, old man! Give me thy hand, away!

    King Lear hath lost, he and his daughter ta'en.

    Give me thy hand. Come on.

GLOUCESTER

    No further, sir; a man may rot even here.

EDGAR

    What, in ill thoughts again? Men must endure

    Their going hence even as their coming hither:

    Ripeness is all. Come on.

GLOUCESTER

    And that's true too.

                    Exeunt. (V.ii.1–11)

After a quick warm-up exercise to aid concentration – the group sat in a circle and sang *Waltzing Matilda* with each student contributing only the next single word as the song went around the circle – the read-through began. I selected two students to read the two parts (mine is a co-educational school and I never worry about gender correspondence) with another to read the stage directions. After the first read-through we had a brief discussion about what was happening in the scene. I find a useful way to gather information is simply to ask 'What do the audience know?' or I use Rex Gibson's excellent questions 'Who? What? Where? Why?' (Gibson 1999: 159–60).[3] This quickly established that the audience know that Lear and Cordelia are about to do battle with Lear's daughters Goneril and Regan, Regan's husband Albany and Edgar's illegitimate brother Edmond. They also know that Edgar is Gloucester's son, but that he is in disguise. Gloucester doesn't know that the person leading him is his son, because he is blind and Edgar disguises his voice. The audience has also seen Edgar trick his father into believing he was saved by a 'miracle' when he tried to kill himself by jumping off Dover cliff.

Another read-through with new readers was then followed by a closer examination of the language. Why does Edgar call Gloucester 'father'? Does he want to give the game away or does Shakespeare need to ensure that the audience remembers the real relationship behind the disguise as Edgar uses a generic term for an old man? Someone noticed that 'old man' later in the scene mirrors the use of 'father'. The group decided that language such as 'good host', 'pray that the right may strive', 'comfort' and 'grace' with their positives in the first half of the scene appear to contrast with 'lost', 'rot' and 'ill thoughts' in the second half with their negatives. Indeed, the scene seems very much to fall into two halves, before and after the battle: initial optimism replaced by deep pessimism.

So far we've just read through and now it was time to 'move' the scene. I pointed out that we can't very well have a blind man 'reading' from the script! I suggested that we again have three 'readers' (the third for the stage directions) and two 'actors' who will simply listen very carefully and try and do whatever the scene requires. Both boys and girls wear ties at my school and I got the student playing Gloucester to take off her tie and her partner blindfolded her with it so she was really blind. This made it easier for the student acting Gloucester and it also helped the observers to see the tentative way the blind Gloucester moves and depends on Edgar.

The question immediately arose, what were we going to do about the Lear/Cordelia procession at the start of the scene? Why is it there and, anyway, what kind of stage is this? We had cleared an open space in the classroom around which the students were sitting and I suggested we should try for the original staging conditions. (If necessary, a quick reminder could happen quite naturally here about the general nature of an open or thrust stage, because the students need to know.) The students discussed how the Lear/Cordelia procession could work on such a stage – they could even demonstrate – and why a visual reminder of an active 'good' party may be necessary at this point. Then the scene with Gloucester and Edgar got under way. Almost immediately, there was a problem. 'Where is the tree?' asked 'Edgar'. I got the class to answer. Some required a realistic prop, other students, remembering that the Elizabethan/Jacobean stage had stage posts, suggested that one of these could be a 'tree', while others again suggested that maybe we were called on to just imagine the tree. (This can be allowed to develop into a discussion about the use of scenery through the ages). We decided that as long as Edgar knew where the tree was, our performance would work. Edgar settled Gloucester under the tree. His exit was awkward. How should Edgar leave the stage? Quickly, suggested someone, he wants to get to the battle which is about to begin. We rehearsed him rushing off with Gloucester's line covering his exit and then running back on, scared of what may follow him.

At this point the fact that Gloucester was left alone on the stage became graphically obvious to the group. When the scene ended, we discussed what a strange and daring bit of theatre this is. The students were used to the idea of Shakespeare leaving a character alone onstage who will then address the audience in soliloquy, but here Shakespeare leaves the character alone and gives him no lines!

In our study of the play we had been noting the recurrent motif of stripping away. Lear loses his daughter Cordelia, his loyal follower Kent, his kingdom and his reason. Edgar loses his inheritance and then strips away his clothes, which will prompt Lear to do the same, and Gloucester loses his eyes. All this was obvious enough. We had also been tracking the way the play's language itself is stripped down, often to very simple negative terms that are repeated over and over – 'nothing' has reverberated through the play. As the play moves to its close perhaps we are even dispensing with language itself!

Someone suggested that the scene was a bit weird because we don't see the battle. I asked the questioner how she felt about this and the answer was 'a bit cheated', because not only did the goodies lose, but we didn't even get to see the fight! I suggested that we hold that thought, because there was something that we had left out – the sound effects.

I pointed to the stage direction 'alarum and retreat within' and suggested that this is theatrical shorthand. Probably, Shakespeare's original audience would have recognised the particular trumpet calls it requires as advance and retreat, but maybe there were other noises too. I suggested that half the group become Lear and Cordelia's army and that I wanted them to make the sounds of defeat and that the other half become Albany's army and from them I wanted the sounds of victory. There was much mirth about this as the two sides worked out just what sounds would be appropriate.

I explained that when we ran the scene again, after Edgar's exit, the noises they were to make would come up and that I would indicate when the noise was to get louder or softer by raising or lowering my arms. The cue for Edgar to come back on would be the noises abating.

We had a quick 'sound effects' practice. The noises they made were mainly shouts and cries – aggression from the victors, death cries and anguish from the losers. At that point I suggested that I wanted the class to pay particular attention to Gloucester when we ran the scene again. I also suggested that Gloucester and Edgar make their entrance from outside the classroom. I went out with them and briefed the blindfolded Gloucester. I suggested to the actor that when Gloucester was left alone on the stage, he should respond to the noises the class was making and that because he was blind he would not know what was happening. I wanted the audience to see how he felt about the noise.

The scene was run and at Edgar's exit, I acted as 'conductor' and the class made their battle noises with gusto. Suddenly, Gloucester sat bolt upright, then crouched down on the ground. I increased the volume of sound. Gloucester crawled away only to find there was no escape and scuttled back like a frightened animal. It was obvious that he was both afraid and confused. The noise died away and Edgar ran back. Now Gloucester's negative responses in the face of Lear's defeat seemed perfectly motivated.

When we discussed what had happened, the class saw that Shakespeare may have given Gloucester no words, but he has given him something to do. To return to our earlier point about stripping away, perhaps we have moved from words to sound – a point we take up in a later class when, in the next scene, Lear enters carrying Cordelia and may make the noise rather than articulating the word 'howl'.

'What do you think the audience are feeling *during* the battle?' I asked. After some hesitation, someone suggested 'confused, because they have no idea what is going on'. 'They are just like Gloucester' offered someone else. We explored the idea that the audience have to experience the battle as the blind man does and that this may be another reason why there is no battle for them to see. I told the class about a famous production by Peter Brook at Stratford in 1962 for the Royal Shakespeare Company. Gloucester was left alone centre-stage and, according to my ear-witness (!), the sounds of battle which were piped around the entire auditorium rose to a deafening level, actually placing the audience *in* the battle.

It was time to return to that thought about the audience feeling cheated. Throughout the play we had been tracking the way Shakespeare creates expectations in the audience and often reverses them. The question I now asked the group was 'What do you think the audience expects to happen in this scene?' The group wasn't sure. 'Well, they wouldn't expect Lear and Cordelia to win or a happy ending, because this is a "tragedy",' suggested someone. Fair enough, I said, but if Shakespeare's contemporaries remembered an older play, *King Leir*, in which Leir and Cordella do win the battle and Leir recovers his kingdom (as he does in nearly all the traditional versions of the story), they might well have expected Lear and Cordelia to win in Shakespeare's version too. If they *were* expecting Lear and Cordelia to win, this is one of the greatest reversals of expectations in the play.

The power of such unfulfilled expectations should not be underestimated, I suggested. In the late 17th century they caused Nahum Tate to rewrite the play so that Lear and Cordelia do win the battle, Lear regains his kingdom and in a 'happy ever after' ending Cordelia and Edgar marry. I pointed out that Tate's version of the play was the *only* one performed for over one hundred and fifty years!

We focused on Gloucester's comments towards the end of the scene. Someone suggested that maybe he was now speaking for the audience who must also be feeling pretty depressed. In our performance Edgar had tried to pull Gloucester to his feet on 'Give me thy hand; come on!' and Gloucester had refused to budge to underline the words: 'No further, sir; a man may rot even here'. We considered this line and Edgar's response: 'What in ill thought again? Men must endure/Their going hence even as their coming hither./Ripeness is all.' We explored the contrast between 'rot' and 'ripeness', noting that here the usual order of growth is reversed (another reversal!). We discussed what Edgar may have meant. Was it that we can't do anything about our birth and we can't prevent our death, so we must put up with life and at least gain some understanding? Or, as Foakes suggests (1977: 363–4), is it more like Hamlet's 'the readiness is all', simply being prepared for death?

We noted that when Edgar first says 'Come on', Gloucester refuses to move, but when Edgar repeats the order after his comment about 'ripeness', Gloucester agrees to go. However, Gloucester gets the last word, 'And that's true too'. I asked what they thought he meant. 'He agrees with what Edgar was saying' suggested someone. 'Not really,' said someone else, 'because he says "that's true *too*" which suggests that Edgar is right, but so is Gloucester's earlier point about "rot".' I explained that some critics, especially those who favour a 'Christian' reading of the play, emphasise the importance of Edgar's lines. The scene does give some warrant for this with its use of 'good host' and 'grace' and Edgar's lines have both a biblical echo and the sound of a pithy aphorism. We tried playing the lines to emphasise this kind of reading, playing down Gloucester's response. Then we tried an emphasis on Gloucester's final words (and although an audience doesn't know it yet, they are his last words in the play), showing his continuing reluctance to move with perhaps a stop and a backward look. We tried to play the ending so that the audience would hear both points of view. Edgar delivered his line with some exasperation, as though not fully convinced, but needing his father to move, and Gloucester spoke the words with absolute conviction and some sadness.

And as the lesson came to a close I suggested to the students that they keep in mind the things we had been exploring in the scene – especially the 'both/and' balance rather than an 'either/or' decision. I asked them to think about choices, confusion and uncertainty as they each work out just how they would perform Lear's final lines, because this would be the focus for our next period.

Objections to the teaching method outlined above may be that it takes a long time to do a very little and that I am actually leading the students towards the meanings I want them to find rather than letting them find their own meanings. I have to agree that it does take a long time, but I would not attempt to treat the whole play in this way. I would select only a few key scenes and/or moments for this type of workshop treatment. The scenes chosen should also demonstrate something about the play as a whole. I hope that the emphasis on performance in the classwork keeps it uppermost in the students' minds in their private study, and homework and class-preparation tasks are designed to maintain this focus. In a similar way, much of the work on critical interpretations, production history and even comparisons of film/video performances should arise out of the performance work and some of this can also be done in their own time. Finally, I admit too that I'm leading the students, but then that's how I see my role as teacher.

Notes

1   The question in the actual exam (October 2001) – 'How might different productions dramatise the struggle between chaos and order in *King Lear*?' – was narrower and more old-fashioned than this sample and the students were correspondingly disappointed. At least the emphasis was still on performance.

2   See the chapters by Drábek (Chapter 11) and Joughin (Chapter 12) for more on the aesthetic response and audience/reader reaction as a departure point for further analysis of a playtext.

3   Gibson is also series editor for the Cambridge School Shakespeare, an excellent series with the focus firmly on performance, and his *Shakespeare's Language* (1997) CUP contains many fine exercises designed for classroom teachers to photocopy.

References:

Bain, E., Morris, J., Smith, R. (1999) *King Lear*, Cambridge School Shakespeare, Cambridge University Press.

Board of Studies NSW (1999) *English Stage 6 Prescriptions: Area of Study, Electives, Texts*, NSW: Board of Studies.

Board of Studies NSW (2000) *2001 English Hisgher School Certificate: Specimin Examination English (Advanced) Paper 2 – Modules*, NSW: Board of Studies.

Cook, Caldwell (1917) *The Play Way*, London: Heinemann.

Foakes, R. (1997) *King Lear*, The Arden Shakespeare, Walton-on-Thames: Nelson.

Gibson, Rex (1999) *Teaching Shakespeare*, Cambridge University Press.

Peat, Derek (1980) 'Teaching Through Performance: an interview with J.L. Styan', *Shakespeare Quarterly* 31.2: 142–152

4

Teaching Shakespeare through Performance

Ted Tibbetts

'My kids will never do that,' I often hear at my Shakespeare workshops. This seems to be the most intimidating factor in using theatre activities to engage students: students won't engage in the activities. To be fair, standing up in front of an audience and attempting to speak a seemingly foreign language can frighten even the most comfortable of public speakers. However, over time a performance approach to Shakespeare will inspire even the most reluctant learners.

This growth became clear to me last fall as I was learning white-water kayaking. I've done a fair amount of whitewater canoeing. The prospect of running rapids in an open boat or on occasion swimming them doesn't pose much of a threat to me. However, a friend of mine has recently introduced me to kayaking. Somehow, while I can swim rapids without much anxiety, being upside down in a boat through whitewater fills me with much trepidation. Several weeks ago, having been thrashed by a whitewater wave, forced to eject from the kayak and subsequently rescued, I found myself less than enthusiastic about the return to the middle of the river. I was more content fiddling around eddy lines and practicing my rolls in the flatwater. After a while my friend suggested that I practice ferrying across the river with him just downriver of the larger waves. After several successful voyages he suggested that I practice some turns out of the eddy line and into the stronger current alongside the waves. Then he suggested a ferry further up in the current, right at the bottom of the waves. After these more successful endeavours, I began to feel more comfortable in the more active water. Moreover, I began to appreciate what my students feel when I ask them to participate in an activity that feels risky to them, but that I take for granted. Using the following strategies to teach Shakespeare may feel risky to teachers as well. Theatre activities are often 'undiscovered countries' for many English teachers. I have found, however, that by learning with my students I have been able to inspire them the most.

Insults

According to one argument, the reason that Shakespeare occasionally spelled the same word differently in varying places of the same play was because he wrote what he heard in his head, and therefore utilised spelling to capture exactly how he wanted the word to sound. The Elizabethans were much more of an oral-based culture than we are today; they went to 'hear a play' while we go to 'see a concert'. It is therefore no wonder that many of our students struggle with the oral aspect of language. Actors, however, use voice as their primary instrument; therefore teachers should dedicate considerable time toward developing their students' abilities to speak powerfully and clearly. When called upon at the beginning of the year, many of my students have responded with mumblings sounding vaguely like my furnace. However, while concentrating on voice exercises throughout my Shakespeare unit, most of these students improve significantly.

Voice exercises can be a difficult sell to students. Lying around on your back, breathing and gurgling nonsense sounds can be disconcerting to anyone – never mind a self-conscious adolescent. However, these kinds of activities can be done. I like to begin with a high energy/low risk activity like 'insults'. The exercise isn't new. You can find Shakespearean insult lists in many places, especially on the Internet. I like to divide my class into four groups and have each group select four insults from the list. Then I establish the criteria for a competition: volume, articulation, and synchronicity. Then we proceed through four rounds of hurling insults at each other. One group begins and I score it on a scale of 1 to 5 and write the score on the board. Each group follows until each group has gone four times and I tally the score and declare an insult-hurling winner.

Students like the energy and aggressive nature of this activity. What's more, they've begun speaking Shakespeare's words with passion! Thirdly, by speaking these words with their group, they can work with these words in a low-profile manner.

Travelling Passage

Like insults, this activity gets everybody involved. Also, it uses both voice and movement to enhance understanding of the text. Provide each of the students with a passage of text. It doesn't matter if everyone has the same text or not. Often I will have students use a monologue on which they are working, a sonnet, or a large passage from the play that we're studying. The students will walk around the room reading their text out-loud. Instruct students to walk while they read, changing directions when they come to a comma, come to a full stop at a period, kneel on a question mark, and jump on an exclamation point. Colons and semi-colons are wild cards; they can be treated as either a comma or a period.

Rather than pausing at the end of the line or rushing through punctuation as they often do, students will get a feel for the rhythm of the thoughts. Moreover, by reinforcing the phrasing of the punctuation through movement, students become more engaged in the language. After students have completed the reading, discuss any discoveries or observations that the students may have. Did they notice their character changing directions often or not? What might that reveal about the state of mind of their character? Did they jump up and down often? Kneel? Were the thoughts of their passage long or short? Did they stop often? How did the actions make them feel? How might these feelings be appropriate to the meaning of the passage?

Silly Sounds

This activity focuses more on voice but is more action-packed than lying around on your back breathing. Don't get me wrong; those activities are vital to anyone wanting to be a great actor, but in my experience, they tend to be a little too esoteric for high school students beginning Shakespeare. This activity, however, employs similar principles.

I do this activity a couple of different ways. Sometimes I have students sit in groups of three and complete the readings. At other times, I have them walk around the room on their own. Grouping students creates a social, less intense atmosphere with fewer repetitions, while having students work on their own creates a more intense atmosphere with more repetitions. If students are working on individual monologues, I ask them to work independently; if the entire class is working on the same text, I often have them work in groups. For the following exercises, if students are in groups, I have them change readers each time they come to a period, question mark, exclamation point, colon or semi-colon. I usually allow one or two minutes for each section of the exercise.

First, I have students read the text with dramatic flourishes and gestures. This allows them to warm up their mouths and minds to the language. Next, I have them 'surf' the text. In doing this, students read while raising the inflection of their voice and reinforcing this inflection with an upward swooping gesture upon reaching a comma, question mark, colon or semi-colon. Students lower their intonation and make an emphatic downward gesture upon reaching periods and exclamation points. This process helps students see the phrasing and the shape of thought which Shakespeare imbeds in the language.

Next, students pronounce only the consonant sounds. For example, 'So shaken as we are, so wan with care/Find we a time for frighted peace to pant' would be read:

'S shkn s w r s wn wth cr/Fnd w tm fr frtd pc t pnt.' I tell students to 'bite' these consonant sounds … they should be able to feel the sensations that the sounds produce in their mouths. Also, I ask students at the end of the exercise what they noticed. Were the consonant sounds sharp and crisp or were they soft and languid? Why did Shakespeare want that effect?

After the consonants students pronounce only the vowels. 'A glooming peace this morning with it brings' becomes 'A ooi ea i oi i i i.' Like the consonants, I ask students what sounds are prevalent and what mood do the sounds create. After the vowels and consonants, students read the passage exaggerating their articulation. Again, I ask students to pay attention to the feeling that the sounds create in their mouths. They should be able to feel their lower lip vibrate on a 'v' sound. They should be able to feel their tongue vibrate on a 'th' sound.

Next, SING!! Yes, some students will vigorously object to this one, but many others will have fun as well. Model for them and continue; often many will get caught up in the energy. Sometimes I give them suggestions: sing it as an opera, as a TV commercial, as a rap, as a country and western song, as a nursery rhyme.

After singing, begin reading in the lowest register voice that the students can manage and over the course of the line rise to the highest register that they can reach, and then work their way back down. Next, students should read in the most outrageous accent that they can muster! (This one is always a favourite.) They can read it in a southern accent, as a German, a New Englander … whatever comes to them! Next, I have students stand absolutely still, pick a spot at the opposite end of the room and deliver the words to that target. I tell them to imagine the words flying to that spot like darts. Then I have them do the same thing in a whisper. Finally, I tell the students to read the passage like they would 'normally', whatever that means to them at this point!

The idea is just to get students comfortable with Shakespeare's words while using their voice. These exercises, making students more aware of their voice, should improve their faithful reproduction of all the sounds expressed in Shakespeare's language.

Character Visualisation

When I first started using performance strategies to teach Shakespeare to high school students, strangely enough, most of the characters resembled high school students! It didn't matter if the character was Lear or Mustard Seed, most of the characters possessed the same mannerisms as headphone toting, Levi-clad ninth graders. I had failed to show them how to access their imaginations in order to become somebody else. Our acting troupe uses this activity at one of the first rehearsals of any show that we do. It creates an opportunity for actors to begin discovering and creating their character. I usually employ the following kind of monologue for this activity:

Lie on the floor on your backs. Flex your toes for several seconds, then relax. (Continue these instructions up the body through the calves, thighs, buttocks, abdominals, chest, arms, neck and head.) *Focus on a couple of deep breaths, and relax. Feel like a pool of liquid on the floor. Visualise the character that you will portray. What kind of person are you? Optimistic or pessimistic? Benevolent or malevolent? What's your social status? Create a visual picture. What colour and style of hair do you have? Skin colour and texture? Eyes? Teeth? Facial features? Clothes? How would you stand? What pose best represents the essence of that character?*

Keeping your eyes closed, stand and strike that pose. What emotions does that pose generate? Experiment with a few variations of that pose until you find one that works. When you're ready, maintain that pose, but open your eyes and peer out at the other characters in your world. How does your character view these other characters? Close your eyes again. Think about how your character would move. Do you march? Slink? Trudge? Limp? Jaunt? What movement is appropriate to the personality of your character? What motivates you to move? Where would you typically go? Visualise your character's walk.

When you are ready, open your eyes and begin walking as your character. Don't acknowledge any of the other characters yet … focus on your own movements. Where are you going? Why do you need to get there? How do you feel about going there? When you are ready, begin to make brief contact with other characters. How would your character do that? Be sure to consider your status. How does your character feel about these other people? Now exchange greetings with other characters. What might you say? How would you say it? When you're ready, find a space and strike your pose again. How does this pose make a statement about your character? How does this pose feel? Slowly lower your character to the floor and go to sleep. What nightly ritual might your character have? Allow that character to melt out of you and return to your normal state.

In a feedback session afterwards, ask:

What discoveries did you make about your characters? How vividly were you able to imagine your character? What did it feel like?

Fifteen-Minute Plays

Some objections regarding Shakespeare's plays stem from the frustration of not understanding the plot of the play. I find this challenge especially prevalent while covering the history plays. For example, before reading *Henry IV Part 1*, it is helpful to understand the events from *Richard II*. The following activity provides a general plot overview for the entire play in an interactive manner.

Write all the main characters of the play onto slips of paper, and either create or obtain a plot summary. For *Richard II*, I construct character cards for Mowbray, Bolingbroke, King Richard, John of Gaunt, Northumberland, the Queen, Bagot, Bushy, Green, and Exton, which creates ten characters. In order for every student to get a part I construct character cards for a Welsh army soldier and a soldier in Bolingbroke's army.

After the students draw the cards I begin reading the plot summary:

At the opening of Richard II, Mowbray and Bolingbroke are involved in a dispute which escalates to a challenge to a duel. However, Richard steps in banishing Mowbray and Bolingbroke. However, John of Gaunt pleads for his son Bolingbroke, so Richard capitulates and banishes Mowbray forever and Bolingbroke for only ten years.

The students who drew those characters then stand up and act out the events. They can speak if they wish when necessary or appropriate (I'll never forget a student's summary of one of Hotspur's speeches from *Henry IV*: 'cut the crap, let's split the map!'). These results are dynamic and often hilarious. At any rate, the students usually render the plot events in a memorable fashion. At the end of the summary, the class can discuss issues or themes which they feel will be significant in the reading of the play.

Noodling around with the Text

Studying the intricate word-play in Shakespeare's texts can often be tedious and decidedly dull for students. This activity, however, involving the entire class, captures the playful spirit of Shakespeare's wordplay.

After discussing puns with the class, have the students look at the opening scene of *Romeo and Juliet* (or any text that involves a verbal duel between characters.) Tell students to identify the puns made by the characters by circling the pun and drawing an arrow to the word that it plays off. For example:

SCENE I. Verona. A public place.

Enter SAMPSON and GREGORY, of the house of Capulet, armed with swords and bucklers

SAMPSON
 Gregory, on my word, we'll not carry coals.
GREGORY
 No, for then we should be colliers.
SAMPSON
 I mean, and we be in choler, we'll draw.
GREGORY
 Ay, while you live, draw your neck out of collar. (*RJ* I.i.1–5)

Do the first seven or eight lines as a class and then have them complete up to line 30 individually or in small groups. This process is valuable because it requires close reading in order to look at what specific words Shakespeare uses that mirror each other. After students complete the circling and arrow drawing, ask for two volunteers to 'perform' this scene. Instruct the performers to read the text aloud. When they come to a word that has been circled and has an arrow leading pointing to another word, they strike the other reader with a soft sponge 'Nerf noodle'. There are, however, only two acceptable points of attack: the back of the shoulder and the hip. Moreover, these 'attacks' are not those of mortal enemies, but of friends engaging in a combative game. The remainder of the class must participate by laughing heartily at each palpable hit. From a pedagogical standpoint, their participation keeps everyone involved, thus developing an understanding for all students. From a class climate standpoint, their participation creates an upbeat, fun energy, and tends to motivate the readers.

After the activity discuss the students' reactions. How is this Nerf duelling appropriate to the scene? How does the act of striking the other character inform the words? How can the sense of dueling be communicated without the Nerf noodles?

Monologue Puppeteer

Unarguably, much of the power of Shakespeare's language comes from the imagery. Yet, students who are kinesthetic or visual learners will often find the verbose descriptions tedious. Therefore, I often use this activity in order to capture the feeling of longer passages.

Select one person to speak the lines, and another student to read and feed the lines to the speaking students. For example, the feeder will stand behind the speaker and read the text approximately one line at a time in a flat, non-interpretive voice. The speaker will then speak the line in his or her best performance voice. As the speaker recites the passage, I act like a puppeteer and summon class members to stand up and act out the images. In *King Lear*, for example, when the speaker says, 'Blow winds, and crack your cheeks', I direct a student to stand and act out the wind blowing. That student continues the dramatisation while the speaker continues: 'You cataracts and hurricanes, spout 'til you have drenched the steeples ...'. Then I summon two more students to act out the actions of the cataracts and hurricanes. All the actors continue their actions until the end of the passage.

The class should then discuss their observations and reactions to the activity. What did the scene look like? What emotions did it generate in the actors? How did the speaker feel watching these images come to life? What mood was Shakespeare attempting to generate? How is this mood appropriate to the present action of the play?

Setting the Scene

Less verbal students may find it difficult to extract the essence of a scene from the text alone at first. Thus, I try to 'set the scene' as we perform in the classroom so that students can immerse themselves in the language, character and situation. This process often involves establishing contexts, invoking the imagination, and employing props.

For example, in teaching the banquet scene in *Macbeth*, I set the scene by setting up several banquet tables, provide as many plates and glasses as possible for props, (perhaps even some food!). I then choose students to play Macbeth, Lady Macbeth, Lennox, Ross, Murderer, and Banquo's ghost. Any student without a title role will assume the identity of a Scottish Lord attending the banquet. Next, I establish the context of the scene through a class discussion. What has happened recently in the kingdom? Which of the lords suspect Macbeth of murdering Duncan? Who suspects but doesn't care? Who's attending only for the free food? Who dislikes Macbeth? How do you feel about Lady Macbeth? Allowing students to think and talk about these ideas provides a better context in which they can better react to the events of the scene.

After laying this groundwork I have the students run the scene. Upon the completion of the scene I ask for general reactions or observations about the scene and facilitate a discussion about student discoveries. Often, students playing Lady Macbeth will say that they were frustrated and embarrassed by Macbeth's outbursts. Some of the lords will echo this sentiment by saying that it was uncomfortable for them to witness Lady Macbeth berate Macbeth. Students playing the Murderer often say that although they were uncomfortable bringing bad news to Macbeth in a room full of Lords, it was also somewhat of a comfort because Macbeth probably would not react too harshly in front of guests.

Although I like to think of my teaching methods as 'Shakespeare through Performance', the more that I think about it, it's more of 'Shakespeare through Experience'. I am less concerned with my students' ability to act as I am their ability to imagine. These activities create opportunities for students with varied learning styles to access and enjoy the language of Shakespeare's plays.

References

Shakespeare, W. (1964), *Romeo and Juliet*, ed. J. A. Bryant, Signet Classics, New York.

5

Digital Shakespeare

INTEGRATING TEXTS AND TECHNOLOGY

Roger Ochse

Whenever I begin teaching a unit or course in Shakespeare, my students tend to respond with a mixture of awe, fear, respect, and bewilderment. These attitudes appear at every level, from introductory to advanced courses. They are even shared by future public school teachers enrolled in my advanced Shakespeare section. What causes these reactions? One reason may be the intimidation factor; after all, Shakespeare has become the touchstone of literary achievement. To study Shakespeare is to take on a mighty task. But the issue goes deeper than the initial responses we are getting from students. The answer, I suspect, lies both in the ways we have been teaching Shakespeare and the perspectives our students bring to the classroom.

Our problem in teaching Shakespeare originates, I believe, in our difficulty developing methodology that accommodates text as performance. Accelerated by new technologies – most notably the Internet and digital audio/video – our concept of the Shakespearean text has been transformed to the point where we have been questioning our teaching practices. How might we engage these technologies while maintaining our traditional focus on Shakespeare's language? Will we abandon the more difficult study of the printed text in favour of the relatively passive viewing of motion pictures? How can we engage our students in the active study of Shakespeare?

Students attuned to digital play stations and sophisticated special effects in the cinema have difficulty imagining the worlds Shakespeare creates in his plays. The energy of Shakespeare's imagination, released through powerful language and stagecraft, can involve audiences intensely in his characters, plots, and ideas (Widdicombe 2002: 151–52). Not accustomed to simple settings combined with dense language, our students are often confused by the rapid development of ideas connected to action. They ask: just what is happening?

Teachers often deal with this confusion by showing performances of the histories, comedies, and tragedies produced for VCR videos and DVDs. With some assistance from the teacher, students can at least engage with the plays, understanding the basics of character, plot, and theme. Studying the strategies filmmakers have employed in adapting Shakespeare's plays to the cinema can challenge students intellectually as much as more traditional approaches (Buhler 2002: 2). Perhaps watching a movie can lead students back to the printed text, but more likely it will substitute itself as the play in their minds and confine them to particular directors' and actors' interpretations. This does not give them the freedom to interpret for themselves. Viewing tapes and DVDs, while lifting the barrier for many students, can also promote passivity. Perceiving this problem, some teachers have their students act out scenes as dramatic readings or full-fledged performances, complete with set designs and costuming. While many of these student representations mimic the movie interpretations, they still move students in the right direction. As we invite students to become characters such as Romeo, Lady Macbeth, or Richard III, we are inviting an interactive experience and collaboration that may well lead our students to deeper understandings of Shakespeare.

Underlying this desire for interaction, for connection, are modes of thinking and awareness that escape traditional approaches to teaching. Rudolph Arnheim (1969: 13) argues that higher intelligence operates at the level of 'visual thinking'. Therefore we are not lowering our expectations when we depart from our language-based teaching methodology to accommodate students who feel more at home in a world of pictures, spatial forms, and symbols. We are, in fact, working in an interactive environment totally akin to Shakespeare's world where ideas and images converge in action. It is our job as teachers to help our students recognize the power they already possess to participate in that dramatic world.

Paolo Freire (1993) takes us a step further in his criticism of the 'banking' concept of education. In banking education, teachers are the 'subject' and students the 'object' of static, meaningless transfers of words that are literally poured from the expert teacher to the waiting, empty receptacle of the ignorant student. This alienating process leads students to memorise and repeat what they 'learn', and then to store the collected data under the pretence it will somehow be useful. Freire (1993: 53) adds: 'Knowledge emerges only through invention and re-invention, through the restless, impatient, continuing, hopeful inquiry human beings pursue in the world, with the world, and with each other'. Released from the oppression of the banking concept, teachers and students enter into a collaborative relationship in the give-and-take world of authentic thinking, 'thinking that is concerned about reality' (Freire 1993: 58).

Freire's ideas provide us with a useful analogy for our predicament as teachers of

Shakespeare. Many of our students regard the printed text as static and lifeless. Lecturing from our positions of authority will only serve to alienate them further. Our students, accustomed to interactivity, 'read' text more visually than their teachers. Any means by which we can encourage their interaction with the dramatic text, including the application of visual media, will help them assert more control over their learning. Experiencing the text in an authentic manner will not only encourage their appreciation, but will enhance their creative and critical thinking. Inevitably they will find themselves working through Shakespeare's dramatic language, the same verbal barrier that at first might have seemed so impenetrable.

Once this barrier is pierced, what finally wins students over is the power of Shakespeare to shape and represent reality. Stories of suffering, joy, jealousy, revenge, love and hatred, arouse universal responses that no student can resist. It seems sad that teachers now seem to be performing remedial work, using technology to help our students access plays they have difficulty reading for themselves. But the fault may lie not in our students but in ourselves. After all, Shakespeare's plays were intended for performance, not to be read as texts outside the context of theatre. Students as visual thinkers possess greater powers than we may recognise in reconstructing the dramatic world of the play. Perhaps we teachers need to understand the fault lines between our ways of thinking and those of our students. One such division consists in technology itself, the linear, verbal, print-based 'text' of the teacher versus the integrated, visual, performance-based 'text' of the student. We must cross this divide to meet our students where they live.

'Technology,' therefore, is the code that separates these different ways of creating and representing reality. In the words of Marshall McLuhan, 'All media as extensions of ourselves serve to provide new transforming vision and awareness' (Murray 1997: 1). If we read Shakespeare, attend a play, watch a DVD, or perform a scene ourselves, we experience a different 'text' – one that is transformed through the medium we have selected. Rather than 'receiving' a text as a passive or benign reader/viewer, we enter and even project ourselves into the text as a collaborator with 'Shakespeare,' in effect transforming the text and ourselves in the process. If media, as McLuhan suggests, are 'extensions of ourselves,' then through any given medium we are both transforming the text and being transformed through it. This process makes us continuously aware of new possibilities. Technology accelerates this process, just as random access memory enables us to project and recall information using a computer. Technology also facilitates interaction with the Shakespearean text in both linear and non-linear, integrated modes as a continuum *and* as a simultaneous event. As students engage the dimensions of language, theatre, and student performance, they experience a liberating and transforming process through which they become self-motivated learners.

Digital Shakespeare: From Theory to Practice

At its simplest, Digital Shakespeare is the integration of digitally recorded experiences into Shakespeare classes. Using a digital camcorder, students tape scenes from plays they are studying for presentation to the class. But Digital Shakespeare is more than this procedure. Students are provided a structure, within which they are controlling production or meaning via the construction of visual text, which gives them a reason to read, to interpret, and to renew the printed text. As they tape, edit, reflect, and process their productions, students develop their creative and critical thinking through a collaborative, problem-solving activity. Digital Shakespeare thereby applies the visual, interactive, and transforming model suggested by Arnheim, Freire, and McLuhan. It eliminates the barrier between antiquated, dense language and the dramatic space. Students understand that what happens in front of a camera is dramatic; thus they are more easily (through the agency of digital technology) to make something of the linguistic code, to internalise and transform it into action that means something to them.

By establishing a continuum of interactivity, engagement, and creation, Digital Shakespeare intertwines three principles: text as language, text as theatre, and text as student performance. While the discussion of these three principles is provided in this sequence, teachers and students need not approach them in this order as they study Shakespeare. Each of these three underlying principles needs to be described in detail.

Text as language engages the printed text as it has appeared in various editions since the quartos and First Folio. It emphasises the reading of Shakespeare and the interpretation of his dramatic language, extended by study of character, theme, historical context, and critical approaches. This principle comes closest to the way we have been taught and how we have been teaching Shakespeare. An excellent choice for approaching the plays through language is the Cambridge Shakespeare series, which features thematic analyses combined with close textual readings. For the tragedies and histories, students are encouraged to discuss issues of kingship, religion, and statecraft, together with the study of characters and their motives, development of plots, and Shakespeare's poetic language. For the comedies, students are introduced to themes of civilisation versus the 'natural' state of humanity, isolation and reconciliation, and the resolution of conflict through the cultural ritual of marriage. The important feature of this principle is its focus on language, which establishes a fluid, suggestive medium through which students of all ages may enter the dramatic world of the plays. Rather than regard the early modern English of Shakespeare as a barrier to understanding, teachers need to immerse their students in the rich vocabulary and metaphorical levels of meaning contained in key moments in plays like *A Midsummer Night's Dream*, *Macbeth*, and *Romeo and Juliet*. Text as language invites closer readings of the printed text, encouraging our students to absorb and internalise it through reading it aloud, looking up words in the glossary and Oxford English Dictionary, memorising passages, and acting out scenes in class.

Text as theatre takes all the presentations and representations of the plays since they were written and merges them into the text we now study. Sources for text as theatre include historical records, prompt books, contemporary accounts, playbills, videos, and DVDs. The Folger Shakespeare and similar case book-format editions include many historical documents. The Norton Shakespeare provides a CD-ROM supplement with many theatre items. Teachers may also view William Phelps's prompt book pages for the Bosworth Field scene from *Richard III* (V.v) at the Digital Shakespeare website (Ochse 2002). Microfilm reels of various prompt books may be ordered directly from the Folger Shakespeare Library (2002). The most available resource for Shakespeare in the theatre is the abundant supply of videotapes produced by the Royal Shakespeare Company and the Hollywood studios. Students may compare the Hamlets performed by John Gielgud, Richard Burton, Mel Gibson, Kenneth Branagh, and Ethan Hawke. DVDs now feature 'out-takes', directors' and actors' comments, and discussions of the musical scores, costuming, and set design. A full discussion of Shakespeare in the cinema may be found in Buhler (2002). Interactive CDs of plays like *Romeo and Juliet* are produced in karaoke format, where students may fill in missing parts and insert themselves into virtual scenes. Significant Internet resources for exploring Shakespeare in performance include: *Hamlet on the Ramparts* (Massachusetts Institute of Technology 2002), *Shakespeare in an Age of Visual Culture* (Folger 2002), and the *Panoramic (360 degree) View of the Globe Theatre* (Globe Theatre 2002).

Text as student performance takes students directly into the plays themselves, where they become Romeo, Viola, or Hamlet. In the process of preparing, taping, editing, and reflecting upon a particular role or scene, they transform the role and become part of the text itself. After studying Shakespeare as language and theatre, teachers can assign or have students select scenes from particular plays. Acting copies in convenient, scene-by-scene format can be printed from the Oxford Shakespeare website (Bartleby.com 2002) or copied and pasted onto a word processor file such as Microsoft Word for subsequent editing. Using a word processor allows students to enlarge the printed text, make changes during production, and save files of each successive change for later analysis. After blocking the scene, it is then rehearsed without and then with the camera, requiring as many 'takes' as necessary to achieve the desired result. Dramatic readings may be performed prior to videotaping a scene, using the camera with the lens cap on, or with a digital tape recorder.

Digital Video Technology

When my Digital Shakespeare experiment began in summer 1999, digital video was considered a 'high-end' computer application. I obtained a Sony VAIO laptop and a

Sony digital camcorder with an IEEE 1394 'Fire Wire' link to capture and edit scenes from Shakespeare taped on the Black Hills State University theatre stage. At present, pre-installed, integrated hardware/software packages for digital video production are available (often at a premium price), but in the IBM platform environment Sony DV-Gate or Canopus EZ-DV editing software can provide a basic solution in a Pentium III computer with at least a 600 MHZ processor speed and a 20 GB hard drive. High-end, 'industrial strength' software like Adobe Premiere 6.0 requires time to learn its many features, but a less expensive, fully-featured alternative like Sony Foundry's Vegas Video 3.0 would do a most acceptable job with less time invested in learning the software. In the Apple world, the recently released iMac features a DV editing system that includes Apple's user-friendly iMovie 2.0 software and a SuperDrive (CD-RW/DVD-R) for burning CDs and DVDs.

Schools without DV technology can use analogue camcorders in VHS or Beta format, which can be played into DV converters made by several manufacturers. Those teachers wishing to skip the computer altogether may tape scenes until one 'take' is ready to play directly through a television monitor. Helen J. Schwartz at Indiana University–Purdue University at Indianapolis has her students borrow camcorders and shoot their own scenes over weekends, bringing them back to class for viewing and editing (Schwartz 2002). Some DV camcorders, like Sony's Digital 8 models, are capable of 'going backward' in capturing analogue tapes from older Hi-8 models. One could argue, however, that DV is becoming so universally available and reasonable in price (some camcorders now cost about $500 US) that using outmoded equipment makes little sense.[1]

Teaching with DV Technology

The advantage of videotaping scenes, as opposed to staging them for the theatre, is two-fold: first, students can shoot scenes until they are satisfied and not have to worry about forgetting lines in front of a live audience; second, they can pre-view their performances, reflect upon them and improve their understanding of the play and their performances at the same time. It is at this point that language, performance, and experience come together to create a dynamic, interactive sense of the Shakespearean text. Depending on the ages and grade level of the students, teachers can adapt their pedagogy to include reviewing the plays as a whole, comparing student productions with films, videos, and DVDs, as the students continue to revise their interpretations.

To demonstrate how this approach can work successfully with younger students, the Alternative Shakespeare class at Sheffield University collaborated with a class of thirty ten-year-old children at the Nether Green School in a project called 'We're Making *Macbeth*' (Blankenship and Murchie 2002). The older students believed their younger counterparts would learn if they could be brought to enjoy Shakespeare. They discovered two principles that made this experiment possible: first, the ten-year-olds seemed to be young enough to possess a naïve enthusiasm for anything fresh and new, yet to be sufficiently mature to have achieved a level of self-control and academic maturity; and second, the play itself contained reinvigorating powers in several key respects:

1   The language within the text resonated with the children in ways that transcended its superficial difficulty; its rich, fluid sounds and rhythms reached them at their developmental level.

2   The basic emotions of the characters – inferiority, envy, selfish desires, guilt and betrayal – are all felt by children as deeply as adults and therefore are closely connected with their life experiences.

3   The text utilises fairy-tale plots and structures, thereby appealing to the imaginative play combined with real human emotions the children would easily engage.

4   Finally, performance operates at the level of the children's experience of creative role-play, reaching into the very nature of play itself.

As the *Macbeth* students concluded their three-week experience, it became clear that they had entered the world of performance, a 'communal undertaking' that connected the intellectual and childlike elements of Shakespeare. Moreover, as the children became 'producers' of the Shakespearean drama, they deconstructed and reconstructed the text through a multi-faceted collaborative interpretation. Their views were found to be just as 'valid' as those of their older peers or their teachers. The resulting 'synergy', compounded by the children's commendable disregard for limitations, resulted in powerful acting, writing, and learning outcomes.

The innovative 'We're Making *Macbeth*' project should encourage Shakespeare teachers at all levels to experiment with the Digital Shakespeare approach to the text, combining language, performance, and experience. Table 1 below provides a list of scenes teachers could assign their students according to age groups. Employing outcomes consistent with developmental expectations, teachers could reasonably expect the younger students (ages 9–11) to engage the kinaesthetic, musical, and spatial dimensions of intelligence. Students in the middle group (ages 12–14) could be expected to reach a technical understanding of staging, plot and character. The more mature group (ages 15–18) could attain levels of critical thinking, including analysis, synthesis, and judgment.

The delightful 'dumb show' in *A Midsummer Night's Dream* (V.i), with its clumsy, literal characterizations, is ideally suited for younger students. Five characters representing 'heroic' figures, beast, and inanimate objects (Pyramus, Thisbe, Wall, Moonshine, and Lion) should appeal to this age group and their audience. Digital video tends to favour one to three characters in a single frame. The technical challenge for Pyramus and Thisbe scene will be to 'frame' the entire cast of characters and then

Table 1: Teaching Scenes by Age Group

Young (ages 9–11)	Intermediate (ages 12–14)	Mature (ages 15–18)
Midsummer Night's Dream (V.i) Pyramus/Thisbe play	*Julius Caesar* (III.i) Murder in the Senate	*Macbeth* (I.v/I.vii) Lady Macbeth and Macbeth
1 Henry IV (II.ii/II.iii) Hal Robbing Falstaff	*Romeo and Juliet* (II.i) Balcony Scene	*Hamlet* (III.iv) Hamlet and Gertrude
Macbeth (I.i/I.iii) Three Witches	*Merchant of Venice* (IV.iii) Shylock's Suit	*Taming of the Shrew* (II.i) Petruchio and Katherina
Hamlet (V.ii) Sword Scene	*Midsummer Night's Dream* (III.ii) 'Catfight'	*1 Henry IV* (II.v) Falstaff Playing Hal
Midsummer Night's Dream (III.i) Titania and Bottom	*Richard III* (III.iv) Death of Hastings	*Twelfth Night* (III.iv) Malvolio Cross-Gartered
Julius Caesar (II.ii) Calpurnia Warning Caesar	*Hamlet* (I.v) Ghost Scene	*Othello* (V.ii) Death of Desdemona
Merchant of Venice (III.ii) The Three Caskets	*Twelfth Night* (I.v) Cesario (Viola) and Olivia	*Romeo and Juliet* (III.v) Love Scene

zoom in on smaller clusters of performers. The other scene from this play (III.i), featuring two characters – the fairy queen Titania falling in love with Bottom the Weaver as a donkey – can be even more effective for digital video. Students ages 12–14 will benefit from the technical challenges of creating the balcony scene from *Romeo and Juliet* (II.i) or the ghost scene from *Hamlet* (I.v). In each case the illusions of night, hastening time, and intense attraction, must be presented convincingly. Considerable preparation will be required to stage and block the scenes, achieve the proper lighting effect, and deliver varying camera perspectives. For the more mature students (ages 15–18) the production of scenes will be more fully integrated into their study of the plays as a whole. At the same time, the DV process should be more student-led, with the teacher serving as an advisor. Teachers could assign a term paper in conjunction with each student's acting, directorial, or production role. Actors would explain their interpretive and editing process in dealing with the printed script; they would summarize the historical performances of the role they have chosen, and they would describe their view of the role as transformed through their video performance.

These brief suggestions provide only hints of the possibilities in Digital Shakespeare. Whether they comprise a single class module or a complete course, teachers can adapt learning scenarios appropriate to their students' needs. It might be best to start simply with less demanding scenes, before taking on tasks that could well end in confusion, frustration, and disappointment. Just shooting a scene and then playing it back to students can be a significant step toward building poise and self-confidence. Shooting from different angles, going outdoors, adding titles and inserting background music, are all technical enhancements that can be postponed in favour of learning and acting scenes well. Moreover, the process furthers experientially guided close reading of the printed text, which deserves priority over technical refinements in the video productions.

Eventually classes will want to post their 'clips' on the World Wide Web as a class or school project. Streaming Internet video clips are now relatively easy to produce using free and universally available plug-ins like Apple Quick Time, Real Player, or Windows Media Player. These formats are ideally suited for short scenes of less than two minutes in duration, but compression software (an option with some plug-ins or available separately in packages such as Terran Media Cleaner Pro) can help render longer clips without requiring viewers to wait unreasonable lengths of time to download the video files. Classes may also wish to create CDs or DVDs of their productions, which will deliver higher quality video for presentation on computers and televisions, or shown via computer projector to larger audiences.

Conclusion

Approaches to teaching and learning Shakespeare have been moving toward McLuhan's idea of transforming experience through media as extensions of ourselves. While we have not entirely freed ourselves of the purely static, manipulative modes presented in many websites, CDs and DVDs, and textbooks (allowing us to explore ready-made documents but not to collaborate with them as co-authors), current trends point the way toward a more interactive vision.[2]

As we develop new methodologies for teaching Shakespeare in our visual media culture, it seems incongruent to employ technology to lead students to the printed text. However, our real objective is to help them directly encounter Shakespeare's dramatic language in the context of theatre through the agency of student performance. The result is a dynamic pedagogy that improves our performance in the classroom while enhancing student appreciation and understanding. 'The play's the thing' through which we engage multiple intelligences – verbal, quantitative, spatial, musical, kinaesthetic, inter-personal, and intra-personal – for learning that involves the whole person. Digital Shakespeare invites students to construct their own learning through authentic experience, to enter Shakespeare's dramatic world through the 'transforming vision' of digital technology, and to discover the power they already possess to alter that world and be transformed in the process. As collaborators with Shakespeare, students and teachers can pursue new opportunities for change that can make a difference in the world beyond the text.

Notes

1   By the time this chapter is in print, these hardware/software recommendations may well be superseded by more powerful and less expensive options. Most important – and basic – is learning the essentials of digital Videography. The best online source (with a companion print magazine) is *DV.com* (2002), which provides product reviews, practical advice, and expert-led discussion groups. Technique can be acquired through first shooting scenes yourself and afterward helping students learn the process themselves. Another magazine, geared toward the home user, is *Computer Video Maker* (2002), featuring ratings of products, advice on how to use light and sound, with an emphasis on ease of use and price.

2   Mythic-Net, a digital multimedia production company (Kerwin and Truett, 2002), has started to combine theatre and technology to create educational opportunities that would excite young people about Shakespeare. The company will produce DVDs as interactive tools that include: textual commentary by well-known scholars; taped interviews with researchers, cast and crew; and printable versions of the text. Performance Shakespeare, a venture of the Open University in collaboration with the BBC Shakespeare Multimedia Research Group (2002), has created a video of three live performances of *King Lear*, with which the student can interact from the perspective of actor, director, and editor. R. L. Widmann, in her Virtual Shakespeare courses at the University of Colorado–Boulder (2002), takes students through various media representations of the Shakespeare repertory and asks them to reconstruct new texts.

References

Arnheim, R. (1969) *Visual Thinking*, Berkeley: University of California Press.

Bartleby.com (2002) *Oxford Shakespeare* [online], Available:
   http://www.bartleby.com/70/index.html [2002, February 6].

Blankenship, E., and Murchie, D. (2002) 'We're Making *Macbeth*' [online], Available:
   http://www.dolphin.org/erik/nethernet/nethertoc.html [2002, February 7].

Buhler, S. M. (2002) *Shakespeare in the Cinema: Ocular Proof*, Albany: State University of
   New York Press.

Computer Video Maker (2002) *Computer Video Maker* [online], Available:
   http://www.videomaker.com [2002, February 6].

DV.com (2002) *DV.com* [online], Available: http://www.dv.com [2002, February 6].

Folger Shakespeare Library (2002) *Folger Shakespeare Library* [online], Available:
   http://www.folger.edu [2002, February 6].

Folger Shakespeare Library (2002) *Shakespeare in an Age of Visual Culture* [online], Available:
   http://www.folger.edu/institute/visual/index.htm [2002, February 6].

Freire, P. (1993) *Pedagogy of the Oppressed*, New Revised 20th Anniversary Edition, translated by
   Myra Bergman, New York: Continuum Publishing Company.

Globe Theatre (2002) *Panoramic (360 degree) View of the Globe Theatre* [online], Available: http://shakespeares-globe.org/virtual-pictures [2002, February 6].

Kerwin, E., and Truett, B. (2002) *New Production Company Brings Shakespeare into the Digital Age with DVD-Lit* [online], Available: http://www1.internetwire.com/iwire/iwpr?id=29141&cat=en [2002, February 7].

Massachusetts Institute of Technology (2002) *Hamlet on the Ramparts* [online], Available: http://shea.mit.edu/ramparts [2002, February 6].

Murray, J. (1997) *Hamlet on the Holodeck: The Future of Narrative in Cyberspace*, Cambridge: Massachusetts Institute of Technology Press.

Ochse, R. (2002) *Digital Shakespeare* [online], Available: http://www.bhsu.edu/artssciences/asfaculty/rochse/digitalshakespeare [2002, February 6].

Open University and BBC Shakespeare Multimedia Group (2002) *The Open University/BBC Shakespeare Multimedia Research Project* [online], Available: http://www.open.ac.uk/OU/Academic/Arts/shakespr.htm [2002, February 7].

Schwartz, H. J. (2002) *Helen J. Schwartz, Ph.D.* [online], Available: http://php.iupui.edu/~hschwart/ [2002, February 6].

Widdicombe, T. (2002) *Simply Shakespeare*, New York: Addison Wesley Longman.

Widmann, R. (2002) *Virtual Shakespeare, University of Colorado at Boulder* [online], Available: http://www.colorado.edu/English/rlw/3000/2002Spr/ [2002, February 7].

6

Shakespeare Reworked

TEXTUAL INTERVENTION STRATEGIES IN THE UNIVERSITY WRITING CLASSROOM

Paul Skrebels

Students embarking on my course Shakespeare Reworked, offered within the Bachelor of Arts degree at the University of South Australia, find themselves confronted with a number of notorious quotations concerning 'the Bard'. There is Ben Jonson's 1623 encomium, part of which forms the title for this collection: 'He was not of an age, but for all time!' (1975: 264). At the opposite pole is George Bernard Shaw's despairing remark made around 1900, 'I hate to think that Shakespear [sic] has lasted 300 years' (Shaw 1946: xxxix). And sitting somewhere between the two is Northrop Frye's coolly rational, yet doubtless still contentious,[1] observation:

> Shakespeare, we say, was one of a group of English dramatists working around 1600, and also one of the greatest poets of the world. The first part of this is a statement of fact, the second a value-judgement so generally accepted as to pass for fact. But it is not a statement of fact. It remains a value-judgement, and not a shred of systematic criticism can ever be attached to it. (1957: 20)

By virtue of their high-school education and their life experiences generally, my students initially are likely also to accept the value-judgement as fact, and pay lip-service at least to the qualities of timelessness and universality of Shakespeare's work immanent in Jonson's words. The net result is that, regardless of whether or not they sympathise with Shaw's attitude, or delight in Edmund Blackadder's giving Shakespeare a swift punch to the jaw on behalf of 'every schoolboy and schoolgirl for the next four hundred years' for the 'suffering you're going to cause' (Curtis & Elton 1999), their sense of awe in the face of Shakespeare's status as a cultural icon leaves them feeling powerless to do much about interrogating that status with anywhere near the detachment of Frye's assessment, let alone giving expression to their own subjectivity in relation to the phenomenon of Shakespeare in the world.

In its small attempt to share around some of the 'wealth' that Shakespeare represents within our culture, Shakespeare Reworked is premised on 1) that 'Shakespeare' is not simply a body of work, but a discursive construct and the repository of important cultural capital, and 2) that this discourse can and should be intervened in, just as it is by those with more obvious interests in exploiting that cultural capital – filmmakers, advertising companies, TV sitcom producers, and so forth. It thus aims to examine the ways in which Shakespeare's plays have been reworked and reproduced over time, to explore the techniques and cultural and historical contexts that inform such represen-tations, and to experiment with ways of reworking Shakespeare. This last involves encouraging students to articulate where and how Shakespeare 'fits' into their own lives, through the use of a specific pedagogy called textual intervention (Pope 1995).

Unlike conventional literary studies or English courses, Shakespeare Reworked is located within the University's Professional Writing and Communication program, which aims to provide students with 'an understanding of the ways cultures and con-texts shape oral and written discourse and communication' (*Calendar* 2002: 316). Its methods are underpinned by the Aristotelian concept of *techne*, where 'art' and the 'artefact' are to an extent defetishised, so that more emphasis is placed on the 'intrinsic aesthetic or crafting that underlies the practices of everyday life' (Cintron 1997: xii). This is an overtly ideological approach to writing whose origins lie in the ideas of theorists such as Walter Benjamin who, in 'The Author as Producer', 'opposes to the romantic notion of a writer's creative genius an artisanal view of authorship as analo-gous to any act of socio-economic production' (Burke 1995: 216–17).

The textual interventionist project advocated by Rob Pope (1995) also stems from both Benjamin's reading of history, as well as Bertolt Brecht's concepts of *Verfremdung* (estrangement) and 'an active *grasping* (*Eingreffung*) of meaning':

> Crucial to both is the critical re-presentation and opening up of that which was assumed to be finished or fixed. For only if we can creatively conceive of a story or history as an interaction that might have been otherwise can we exercise our critical judgements as to the implication and consequences of the actual hi/story as told or enacted. Such acts of 'making strange' and 'grasping' meanings are thus morally and politically charged. (Pope 1995: 189)

Textual intervention involves trying to understand how a text works literally by playing around with it: 'to intervene in it in some way (large or small), and then try to account for the exact effect of what you have done' (Pope 1995: 1). It is therefore based on the assumption that interpretation/reading/meaning-making is a rhetorical process, where there is always a dialogic (indeed, a 'triadic') relationship between writer, text and reader. Not only do writers 'play the role of the reader' in 'positioning their texts in ways that will somehow appeal to readers, ... in effect, writ[ing] those readers into being' (Seitz 1992: 145), but readers also 'persuade themselves that a particular reading of a text is preferable to others' (1992: 147). In charting the same theoretical territory, Ian Reid observes that 'reading, too, is a craft of composition, a practice of frame-making that overlaps with the artist's creative labour' (1992: 16). And so, extrapolating from Benjamin on authorship via the thoughts of Seitz, Reid and others on reading, Pope is able to claim that,

> Approaching texts as an 'artisan', as a 'craft/wo/man', means that you treat them with respect – but also the no-nonsense directness and systematicness – that a skilled engineer or dressmaker approaches their materials and the immediate task in hand. (1995: 3)

Textual intervention therefore provides a means of linking critical theory with classroom practice – and thus creating a form of 'literary praxis' – with the potential for producing what John Trimbur calls 'socially useful knowledge' (2000: 191). Shifting Shakespeare out of the realms of traditional 'Eng. Lit.' and into the writing class – turning what Barthes would term 'readerly' texts into 'writerly' ones (Hawthorn 1998: 192–93) – places Shakespeare back into the world at large and puts him to work in helping students to become producers as well as 'consumers' (in all the possible senses of that term). Rather than destroying Shakespeare's status, the explicit ideological agenda of the textual interventionist project and of courses such as Shakespeare Reworked actually reinvigorates him in the lives of students by putting him back in their world(s) also. They become confident enough to treat Shakespeare as *their* cultural capital as well as that of the RSC, the Branaghs, Luhrmanns, and anyone else currently getting returns out of it.

The remainder of this chapter will therefore take its cue from the two main activities undertaken in the Shakespeare Reworked class, and examine: 1) the way Shakespeare's work has been intervened in by a particular practitioner, and to what effect; and 2) the ways students might engage in similar activities for particular purposes of their own.

The Rest is Silence: an intervention into *Hamlet*

Many existing cultural products hitherto at best marginalised by, but more often omitted from, traditionalist literary studies courses find a place within the Shakespeare Reworked syllabus. In particular are those works Rosenthal terms 'variants', 'which retain the Bard's plots and characters without using his poetry or settings' (2000: 8),[2] such as Helmut Käutner's 1959 film *The Rest is Silence*, a fascinating if rather neglected variant of *Hamlet*.[3] Käutner (1908–1980) was a mainstream German filmmaker whose prolific output from the 1940s to the 1970s included some films such as *The Devil's General* in 1954 and *The Captain from Köpenick* in 1956 (*Helmut Käutner* 2001), which investigated what was then West Germany's place in the world in terms of its militaristic and subsequently Nazi past. *The Rest is Silence* is a contemporary reworking of *Hamlet* that uses the plot of the original as a means of carrying out just such an interrogation of recent German history. Its title – from Hamlet's final words in the play – refers primarily to the conspiracy of silence over the role played by German industry in the rise of the Nazi war machine.

The storyline begins with John Claudius's return to Germany after 20 years in America. He is heir to the Claudius Steelworks following the suspicious death of his father, but his mother Gertrud has since married his Uncle Paul. Obsessed with finding the truth, John not only rejects his childhood sweetheart, Fee, but accidentally kills her father. He discovers that Paul killed his father, and that the firm was involved in the Nazi armament program, but that its problematic past has been forgotten by the occupying powers and the present government in the interests of its services to the Cold War effort. Along the way John uses a contemporary dance production of *The Mousetrap* to 'catch the king', and turns the tables on the Rosencrantz and Guildenstern equivalents (two members of the dance company) charged with getting him committed to a mental asylum in England.[4] John reveals his findings, but here the film breaks away from the original plot by having Gertrud kill Paul herself, and ending with John watching helplessly as Fee is committed to an asylum while the police arrive for his mother.

Käutner's intervention is an excellent exemplar for the Shakespeare writing class. Obviously, it serves as a springboard for looking at the relationship non-anglophone cultures have with Shakespeare.[5] More practically, however, it provides easy access to the original play, given its updated setting and language (once subtitled for the non-German speaker, of course), and an insight into the extent to which the plot and storyline remain valid and adaptable for contemporary audiences. Examining these effects leads in turn to a deeper significance, though. Over time, inevitably, the immediacy of the social and political contexts within which a play such as *Hamlet* was first produced and received have dissipated. 'Classic' productions of Shakespeare, preoccupied with maintaining a 'Shakespearean' aesthetic, tend (consciously or unconsciously) to erase or elide the more overt ideological aspects of the originals. Thus, for example, both the Olivier (1948) and the Zeffirelli (1990) versions of *Hamlet* present claustrophobic psychodramas that omit the wider world of power struggle and 'dirty' politics of which Elsinore is only a small part.

The Rest is Silence, on the other hand, squares up to the issues of power and corruption, totalitarianism and capitalism, and of facing one's individual and collective past, all of which are constitutive of the Shakespeare text, and which are activated to varying degrees in the more inclusive efforts such as Branagh's full-length presentation (1996) and Almereyda's 'postmodern' interpretation (2000). But, I would argue, even these latter admirable projects are in danger of swamping the issues and overpowering a modern audience. Such 'original text' productions of Shakespeare still tend to be complicit in the 'uneven distribution of cultural capital' (Trimbur 2000: 198) associated with the what Benjamin terms the 'cultural treasure' (1997: 192), before whose hallowed status the student stands in awe.[6] The result can be a form of *aporia* – a creative and critical 'brick wall' – that separates the students, with their particular history, from the supposed 'universality' of Shakespeare.

Variants such as *The Rest is Silence*, on the other hand, treat the cultural treasure with the sort of 'cautious detachment' advocated by Benjamin (1997: 192), and which, as we have seen, forms the basis of the textual interventionist method. Käutner's film restores Benjamin's 'time of the now' (1997: 192) to *Hamlet* by giving the play not only a very precise cultural, social and political context, but a reworked text to suit that context. This in turn gives us some inkling of the 'nowness' it may have had in Shakespeare's own time that has since been lost to us. Paradoxically, then, the very 'anti-universality' of *The Rest is Silence* actually exposes *Hamlet* as an ideological text (as opposed to the hidden ideologies supporting its representation as a 'classic', apparently apolitical, play). Käutner's intervention and others like it free up Shakespeare: no longer fixed, self-contained and closed off as a cultural treasure – preserved under glass, as it were – his value as cultural capital for our students can only increase.

Student interventions

Exploring a film such as *The Rest is Silence* encourages students to see that Shakespeare can 'belong' to the (re-)writer under their own terms, and that those terms are nothing less than the specificities of one's own place in a given culture at a particular historical moment. Here, then, are four examples of particularly effective interventions by students in Shakespeare Reworked who have demonstrated a firm grasp of that idea. The task itself involves students taking a scene from a Shakespeare play, reworking it in any way they see fit, then justifying their decisions in a commentary accompanying the intervention. Regrettably but necessarily, the examination of each will be brief.

Terry Glouftsis touts his 'Confrontation at Dunsinane' as a presentation of 'Marvel Comics and DC Comics … in conjunction with Immortal Bard Comics', starring The Incredible Hulk as Macbeth, Superman as Macduff, Access as Malcolm, Batman as Old Siward and Captain America as Ross (Glouftsis 2001: 1). It features beautifully drawn and coloured renditions of the comic superheroes playing out *Macbeth* V.viii, the final scene, with gestures appropriate to the words.

In his commentary, Glouftsis quotes Lloyd Davis to the effect that 'any response to Shakespeare, from popularity at the box office to a new series of academic studies, represents a certain kind of theoretical and cultural investment in what Shakespeare might mean' (Davis 1999: 24). He then tracks his own creative thought processes in devising his comic-book intervention, beginning with the fascinating and very insightful connection between *Macbeth's* traditional associations with bad luck by theatrical people (who call it, superstitiously, 'the Scottish play') and the run of 'catastrophes' associated with 'the history of Superman productions':

> George Reeves (the first television Superman) suicided, Christopher Reeves is a paraplegic after falling from his horse, Margot Kidder (Lois Lane) has had numerous mental breakdowns, Dean Cain (latest Superman) almost died in a motorcycle crash, Teri Hatcher (latest Lois) almost died in childbirth, etc. The list goes on to production reels being lost, finance collapsing, production crew dying and the latest Superman movie being pulled because of too many legal entanglements. (Glouftsis 2001: 9)

Glouftsis is able, therefore, to draw stimulus for his intervention from two apparently disparate yet well entrenched sets of cultural associations – he could not, for example, 'in good conscience cast Superman as the villain' Macbeth (2001: 9) – in order 'to present the play in a way familiar to many teenagers', because 'it is in teenage years that Shakespeare is thrust at students' (2001: 10). At the same time, his version underscores the cultural status accrued to Shakespeare, who 'is considered so powerful he has become mythical, a Superhero' (2001: 10). His own evaluation, that his intervention into *Macbeth* 'is less about the actual play than the way it and the author are perceived' (2001: 10) is perceptive if somewhat self-effacing, given the degree of skill his work reveals in 'blocking' or 'storybooking' *Macbeth* V.viii, and therefore in understanding how the scene works in practice.

Nick Atanasoff's 'Cheech and Chong do Donalbain, or: How I learned to stop worrying and love the bong' takes intervention into *Macbeth* a stage further by not only transposing Act II, scenes i–ii to an updated setting, but rewriting the language into Atanasoff's own crazy variation of blank verse. The result is clever, very funny, and splendidly vindicated in his commentary. He says, 'I first thought to write in the style of comedy as I was watching *Whose Line Is It Anyway?* The crowd, as they so often do, shouted "Do Shakespeare" … It's so *ingrained*! And as I read my favourite scene from The Scottish Play it just occurred to me … to turn the title character into Cheech and his wife into Chong" (2001: 19). So, for example, the 'Is this a dagger which I see before me' speech (II.i.33–41) becomes

CHEECH

Is this a cone-piece I see before
me, the handle toward my hand?
Come, let me tote thee. I've
smoked thee not, and yet I want
thee still. Art thou not, induced
vision, sensible to feeling as to
sight? Or art thou but a drugger
of the mind, a mull creation,
proceeding from the heat-oppressed
bong? I see thee yet, packed in as
bum-suckable as this at which now
I draw. (Atanasoff 2001: 5, original lineations)

Atanasoff is not so naïve as to think his efforts are totally original, but he is aware nevertheless that intertextuality operates at many levels and represents an ongoing cultural activity. Of the 'dagger' speech, he comments:

I know this speech has been manipulated before (and probably in somewhere near the same context!), but it's just so easy and enjoyable to do. I'm most appreciative to Shakespeare for putting in the line, 'As this which now I draw'. (2001: 20)

He peppers his speeches with intertextual references of his own: using an actual line from 'Cheech and Chong's infamous Drive-In Sketch'; paraphrasing Edgar Allen Poe with 'a knocking at my chamber door. Nevermore'; and having Chong accuse Cheech 'of being "lost so poorly in your thoughts", which is "more of a Hamlet thing"' (Atanasoff 2001: 21).

Atanasoff is also aware that Shakespeare is 'literature's freak' – the equivalent of 'Mozart, Einstein and Bradman … in the other pursuits of humanity' – yet 'most of my friends have never read a Shakespeare play', and neither had he before taking Shakespeare Reworked (2001: 17–18). With characteristic wit he says it 'was a strange honour to butcher *Macbeth* into a Cheech and Chong X-rated masterpiece', and that it was 'fun, eye-opening and daunting all at once' (2001: 21). To which he might have added that his reworking depended upon an impressive mastery of the original text and a clear understanding of both its actual and potential significance.

Natalie Koumides' 'King Lear and I' represents a more radical intervention still. She believes that 'Ben Jonson's assertion that Shakespeare is "not for an age; but for all time" might be true if we are talking in terms of theme, character and plot', but is 'questionable' when applied to the language itself (Koumides 2001: 10). She therefore presents an intervention into the opening of *King Lear* I.i in the form of a filmscript depicting a small boy, Michael, who, staying with his grandmother, is forced to resort to her bookshelf when the TV breaks down. He discovers the plays of 'shak-sper', and when informed that 'he wrote beautiful, poetical words and his plays are timeless' (2001: 2), wants to know more. Grandma warns him that even so, 'Many people … don't understand his words' (2001: 3), then starts reading from *King Lear*. Koumides cleverly has the film cut to re-enactments of the play in 'authentic' clothes and language when the play is being 'read', and back to Michael and Grandma in between. Michael interjects with, 'No wonder adults don't understand this!' (2001: 4), at which the 'play' switches to a paraphrase of the original in an updated, although still appropriately formal, idiom.

Koumides' intervention works on (at least) two levels. Firstly, it is very finely crafted as a filmscript: it is written to 'industry standards', with correct layout and scene changes, and is well paced and funny in terms of content. For instance, when the 'play-within-the-film' lapses back into original 'Shakespearean', Michael's objection occurs thus:

```
        LEAR
    [...] while we unburthen'd crawl
    towards death.
He takes another breath about to speak when we hear MICHAEL'S
voice and LEAR looks around to see where it is coming from.
        MICHAEL (V.O.)
    Grandma ...


INT.            GRANDMA'S HOUSE                    DAY
    ... they're talking like that again!
        GRANDMA
    Oh, sorry.
```
(Koumides 2001: 7)

Secondly, it raises important questions about what Trimbur terms the 'shift in modality' (2000: 213) between 'authentic' playtext and 'derivative' filmscript. Koumides herself quotes Peter Hall to the effect that Shakespeare is often 'bad screen writing. A good film script relies on contrasting visual images. What is spoken is of secondary importance' (Koumides 2001: 9). What then are the 'rhetorical transformations' (Trimbur 2000: 213) entailed when Shakespeare is transferred to the screen? Is it always a matter of 'dumbing down' the content and language? Koumides states that her aim is to make Shakespeare's plays 'understandable and non-intimidating for new audiences' (2001: 9); note that she has opted for the play-within-the-film device as a means to achieve this rather than an unmediated bowdlerisation into updated English. Clearly her aim is as much to educate as to entertain, as it is to 'illustrate the generation gap and the different approaches each character has because of this' (Koumides 2001: 9). Ultimately, we are left wondering whether Shakespeare has always relied upon 'popular' versioning for its survival, for as Koumides warns, '*As long as Shakespeare remains important*, there will continue to be interpretations of his work and people will invent even more radical ways of adjusting it to fit our changing cultural needs' (2001: 10, my emphasis).

Finally, as a way of illustrating just how radical those ways might be, is Kathryn Hummel's startlingly original intervention, '*Much ado about nothing*: The SMS version'. Hummel takes the first 'French scene' of *Much ado* II.i, where Beatrice discusses her attitudes towards men and marriage with her uncles Leonato and Antonio, and turns it into a text message conversation between a modern young woman, B, and her gay clubber friend, Tony. Hummel admits that she originally 'had very little knowledge of the SMS language' (Hummel 2001: 8), and provides a two-page glossary of Short Message Service language (SMS) sent via mobile phone to help the reader interpret her piece. And it's a good thing she does, as this extract, the equivalent of Beatrice's answer to Leonato's 'Well, niece, I hope to see you one day fitted with a husband' (*Much ado* II.i.52ff) shows:

[Tony]
YBS! AL1Wans is 2 B gr%ving @ YR wedding
[B]
I'll have D party w/o D gr%m 2 make U:-) Men R Scum & treat U like dirt, esp my X. Luv scum? MayB. Marry scum? No Thx. EOL.
(Hummel 2001: 4)[7]

Hummel cites Anne Waldron Neumann's observation about 'the vast difference between reading Shakespeare and the way young people are viewed as consuming culture in today's society; that is, through "film, rock music, advertising, and cyberpunk"' (Hummel 2001: 7) in defence of her intervention. But she makes another very telling observation, besides the obvious one of making Shakespeare relevant to a generation of young people 'besotted with the facility' of SMS on their indispensable mobile phones (2001: 7). Citing Lloyd Davis (1999) and a website called 'Freespeling[sic].com', she says how Shakespeare's work was written 'at a pivotal period' in English cultural history, 'before spelling got fossilised' (Hummel 2001: 8). She implies that we are at a pivotal period ourselves, and that while SMS is just another sign of 'the crisis of dealing with Shakespeare in a time where his work is sometimes regarded as not pertinent', it may also be one of the means by which the crisis 'can be overcome' (2001: 9). Certainly she believes that 'Shakespeare's importance as a literary figure and the genius often displayed in his work is reason enough to make the attempt' (2001: 9). I venture to suggest that the spark of genius exhibited in Hummel's own work, which brilliantly evokes and encapsulates a whole network of contemporary cultures – feminist, gay, clubbing, technological – is reason enough for putting Shakespeare to work in the writing class and seeing what can be done with him in the 21st century.

Conclusion

The excellence of the student work described above notwithstanding, no doubt many – teachers, scholars, and even other students – would regard these activities as exercises based on the sort of warped logic expressed by Mr Puff, the playwright in Sheridan's 1779 play, *The Critic*.[8] When queried over a line in his play (within the play), that 'there is something like it in *Othello*', Mr Puff replies:

> Gad! now you put me in mind on't, I believe there is – but that's of no consequence – all that can be said is, that two people happened to hit on the same thought – And Shakespeare made use of it first, that's all. (1975: III.i.108–12)

But of course, as students discover, Shakespeare was not the point of origin for the majority of his own work, derived as it was from the writings of Plutarch, Holinshed, Cinthio, Saxo Grammaticus, and others. Further, as Gary Taylor wittily and eloquently demonstrates, particularly in his demolition of *The Comedy of Errors* in comparison with its source text, Plautus's *Menaechmi*, Shakespeare 'by no means exhausts the moral universe' (1990: 404), and neither does he take the drama in every direction it might go.

If anything, then, these student interventions chart some of the territory that Shakespeare dared not venture into, and in the process lead us towards a better grasp of the originals themselves:

> We can understand what Shakespeare did only if we understand what he didn't do and understand too that what he didn't do was worth doing. (Taylor 1990:388)[9]

Such an apparently contradictory attitude highlights the bigger contradiction underpinning our relationship with Shakespeare generally. We recognise and acknowledge his greatness and his centrality to our culture, yet we continually reinterpret, rework and exploit his work for all we can get out of it.[10] Ultimately, therefore, the hubristic Mr Puff is on to something. But while I don't think I'm as blasé about Shakespeare's work as Mr Puff, nor as necessarily scathing as Taylor must be in order to make his point, nevertheless I am confident in the capacity of courses such as

Shakespeare Reworked for exposing the inherent contradiction in our relationship with Shakespeare and, via the textual interventionist method, for providing students with the opportunity to take advantage of where that contradiction might lead.

This same inner tension between respect and a refusal to be overawed is symptomatic of the 'utopian esthetics' (Ryan 2001: 229) which inform Shakespeare's Gonzalo, in delineating his ideal commonwealth in *The Tempest*, to assert the need to 'by contraries/Execute all things' (1964: II.i.143–44), and which drive Marxist critics' insistence on brushing history against the grain. In its practical manifestation, such an aesthetic has resulted in many great reworkings of Shakespeare, which Fred Inglis sums up delightfully in his vision of

> radical Schiller translating Shakespeare into *Sturm und Drang*; Verdi turning Shakespeare into opera for the Risorgimento; Kozintsev taking Pasternak's translation of *King Lear* and turning it into his incomparable work in the bleak, ice-cold hills of the Ukraine.
>
> Each man had a drastically non-formalist version of Shakespeare to tell his people. In a primary, intuitive motion of mind they had a work of art … to match with an historical moment. Their intense concern was to fit the story to the history of their side of the historical divide. They sought, in other, more technical words, to hold a balance between art object and local experience without giving the prize to either.
>
> That is the balancing act which ought to be the real foundation of a socialist pedagogy … (1991: 66–67)

Whether Gonzalo's ideal commonwealth or a Marxist socialist utopia are realistic or even desirable goals is less at issue here than that we as teachers, with our implicit faith in 'the contribution of [Shakespeare's] drama to the civilizing process' (Ryan 2001: 230), continue opening up ways for our students to share in the cultural capital that is Shakespeare, and to make of it what they will.

Notes

1 See, for example, Taylor (1990: 377–80), who discusses and in turn refutes Harry Levin's 1973 rebuttal of Frye's assessment.

2 The debate as to whether such works constitute 'Shakespeare' at all will, I trust, be resolved to some extent by the discussion that follows, and is one that will almost inevitably arise (and should not be avoided) in one's own classroom.

3 Thus in Rosenthal's recent overview of screen Shakespeares, Käutner's film is missing from the discussion of versions of *Hamlet* (2000: 18–21). This is despite the fact that in many ways *The Rest is Silence* is a 'natural' antecedent of Michael Almereyda's 'postmodern New York' *Hamlet* (2000), starring Ethan Hawke.

4   Here Almereyda's apparent debt to Käutner's version is particularly marked. Both films have their Hamlet foiling the Rosencrantz and Guildenstern plot on board an aeroplane bound for England.

5   Particularly the long history of German fascination with and appropriation of his work, to the extent of regarding him as *unser Shakespeare*. The film also lends itself to a discussion of metanarrativity and the issues of the life/art dichotomy, in the clever casting of Hardy Kruger as Hamlet, an 'international' actor whose career abroad is akin to both Hamlet's time away in Wittenberg and John Claudius's in America.

6   See, for example, Denise Albanese's comment about Branagh's *Hamlet*, that this 'lavish and prestigious film embodies an increasingly regressive notion of cultural capital that is ... associated with the literary legacy of Great Britain. In this regressive dispensation, the obvious value of *Hamlet* is that it be filmed with reverence' (2001: 210).

7   Translation: [Tony] 'You'll be sorry! All one wants is to be grooving at your wedding.' [B] 'I'll have the party without the groom to make you happy. Men are scum and treat you like dirt, especially my ex. Love scum? Maybe. Marry scum? No thanks. End of lecture.'

8   Itself a reworking of an earlier play, Buckingham's *The Rehearsal* (1671).

9   Conversely, Albanese maintains that reading, for example, Kurosawa's films 'as evidence of Shakespeare's infinite translatability elides what is *not* Shakespearean' in such interventions (2001: 208).

10 The fundamental tenet of Taylor's 1990 thesis is that Shakespeare's continued place in our culture *depends* upon his being continually reinvented from one age to the next. Such an assertion (to which I am obviously rather partial) would serve to push a course like Shakespeare Reworked from the margins of Shakespeare study towards its centre.

References

Albanese, Denise (2001) 'The Shakespeare film and the Americanization of culture', *Marxist Shakespeares*, ed. Jean E. Howard and Scott Cutler Shershow, London and New York: Routledge, 206–26.

Atanasoff, Nick (2001) 'Cheech and Chong do Donalbain, or: How I learned to stop worrying and love the bong', unpublished student paper, University of South Australia.

Benjamin, Walter (1997) 'Theses on the philosophy of history', *Revolutions of the word*, ed. Patricia Waugh, London: Arnold, 191–93.

Burke, Seán (1995) *Authorship: From Plato to the postmodern*, Edinburgh: Edinburgh University Press.

Calendar (2002) Adelaide: University of South Australia.

Cintron, Ralph (1997) *Angel's town*, Boston: Deacon Press.

Curtis, Richard, and Ben Elton (1999) *Blackadder back and forth*, Tiger Aspect Productions.

Davis, Lloyd (1999) 'Shakespeares: Critical/cultural/multiple', *English in Australia* 125 (August), 14–25.

Frye, Northrop (1957), *Anatomy of criticism: Four essays*, Princeton University Press, Princeton.

Glouftsis, Terry (2001) 'Confrontation at Dunsinane', unpublished student paper, University of South Australia.

Hawthorn, Jeremy (1998) *A concise guide to contemporary literary theory*, 3rd ed, London: Arnold.

Helmut Käutner (2001) The Internet Movie Database, http://us.imdb.com/Name?K%E4utner,+Helmut (accessed 9 February 2001).

Hummel, Kathryn (2001) '*Much ado about nothing*: The SMS version', unpublished student paper, University of South Australia.

Inglis, Fred (1991) 'Recovering Shakespeare: Innocence and materialism', *Shakespeare in the changing curriculum*, ed. Lesley Aers and Nigel Wheale, London and New York: Routledge, 58–73.

Jonson, Ben (1975) 'To the memory of my beloved, the author Mr William Shakespeare: and what he hath left us' (1623), *The complete poems*, ed. George Parfitt, Harmondsworth: Penguin, 263–65.

Koumides, Natalie (2001) 'King Lear and I', unpublished student paper, University of South Australia.

Pope, Rob (1995) *Textual intervention: Critical and creative strategies for literary studies*, London and New York: Routledge.

The Rest is Silence (1959) [orig. title *Der Rest ist Schweigen*] Helmut Käutner (dir. and writ.), Freie Film Produktion GMBH.

Reid, Ian (1992) *Narrative exchanges*, London: Routledge.

Rosenthal, Daniel (2000) *Shakespeare on screen*, London: Hamlyn.

Ryan, Kiernan (2001) '*Measure for Measure*: Marxism before Marx', *Marxist Shakespeares*, ed. Jean E. Howard and Scott Cutler Shershow, London and New York: Routledge, 227–44.

Shakespeare, William (1964) *The Tempest*, The Arden Shakespeare, ed. Frank Kermode, London: Methuen.

Shaw, George Bernard (1946) Preface, *Three plays for Puritans*, Harmondsworth: Penguin, vii–xxxix.

Sheridan, Richard Brinsley (1975) *The Critic* (1779), *Sheridan's plays*, ed. Cecil Price, Oxford University Press, London.

Seitz, James E. (1992) 'A rhetoric of reading', *Rebirth of rhetoric: Essays in language, culture and education*, ed. Richard Andrews, London and New York: Routledge, 141–55.

Taylor, Gary (1990) *Reinventing Shakespeare*, London: Hogarth Press.

Trimbur, John (2000) 'Composition and the circulation of writing', *CCC: The Journal of the Conference on College Composition and Communication* 52 (2): 188–219.

7

Teaching *The Tempest*

ONE TALE, MANY TEXTS

Mary T. Christel

As the teaching of plays from Shakespeare's canon has come under greater scrutiny and is increasingly deemed irrelevant to modern students, teachers need to consider how a text like *The Tempest* has been part of a lively process of reinvention and response for the last two hundred years. What compelling questions does this text pose to poets, dramatists, and filmmakers, spurring them on to creating adaptations that comment on diverse cultures, characters, and conflicts that continue to resonate the seminal themes of this rich source material? By combining the study of Shakespeare's romance with a poem, a play and a film – all inspired by the same tale born out of the Renaissance – this chapter will illustrate the continuing relevance and appeal of the work to contemporary students.

The enduring appeal of *The Tempest* finds its source in the persistence of an imperialistic mentality that has coloured many periods of history since Elizabethan England. The cry of the oppressed is explored in Robert Browning's 19th century poem, 'Caliban on Setebos'. Prospero's dominion over the island and its native inhabitants through his supposed superior and enlightened knowledge and experience finds expression in Aimé Césaire's *A Tempest*, a dramatic adaptation that gives voice to the negritude movement of the 1960s. The enlightenment that Prospero gains through the unlikely tutelage of his fairy minion, Ariel, on the value of human compassion and forgiveness, is illustrated in Paul Mazursky's film *Tempest*, when a successful New York architect escapes the tyranny of the world he has created to find refuge on a remote Greek island. Through 19th and 20th century poetry, modern drama, and contemporary film, the continuing conversation initiated by Shakespeare regarding imperialism, revenge, compassion, and forgiveness brings his tale even closer to modern readers.

In examining adaptations of any type of source material, the study must be framed by an analytical process that addresses the unique endeavour of adaptation. The essential themes of the source material must be identified as the 'heart' of the text. Then the characteristics of setting and essential events of the plot create the skeleton that can be further fleshed out with the key characters and their unique relationships to one another. The previous paragraph has identified those themes that should operate in whole or in part at the centre of any type of adaptation of Shakespeare's play. The setting of an adaptation of *The Tempest* doesn't necessarily require a deserted island; any environment, either physical or psychological, that isolates the protagonist from mainstream society at large could be used. The basic plot structure of *The Tempest* includes the initial shipwreck and stranding of a father and daughter, the subsequent conjuring of a storm for a second vengeful shipwreck, the tensions between Prospero and Caliban and Ariel, who both seek their freedom, the maturing of a beloved child, and the reconciliation between Prospero and his foes from both the civilised and savage worlds he has inhabited. The social relationships that flesh out the plot involve master and slave, father and child, and king and subject. Another archetype that intrigues adaptors of this tale is the tension between natural and civilised states of existence as portrayed through Miranda, the innocent child, as well as through Caliban, the natural inheritor of the island and the captive of both Prospero and the clowns, Stephano and Trinculo.

The following set of questions can further focus the analysis of adaptations:

- What is the modern poet's, playwright's, or filmmaker's purpose in using Shakespeare's *The Tempest* as source material for their own work?
- Which of the essential setting or plot elements are immediately recognisable in this adaptation? What are the essential setting or plot elements that must be included in an adaptation to evoke the source narrative?
- Which characters are essential to the development of the adaptation? Why have these characters been selected to be at the foreground of the adaptation? How are they similar to or different from their prototypes in Shakespeare's play?
- Which images, motifs, symbols, or metaphors are central to the source's meaning or dramatic development? To what extent are those elements retained, eliminated, or modified in this adaptation?
- Which choices made by the writer or filmmaker are the most successful in translating the original literary source to another medium? Which choices are the least successful and why?
- How does the modern adaptor use the resources and conventions of poetry, drama, or film to make this adaptation both a response to the original Shakespearean text and a unique creative expression of the modern adaptor's vision and purpose?

With these tools for examining and evaluating an adaptation, a teacher can set to the task of selecting specific works to complement any number of approaches to teaching Shakespeare's romance. What follows are a range of choices of adaptations suitable for any number of student abilities and interests.

Connections to 19th and 20th Poetry

During the 19th and by the mid 20th centuries the major responses to *The Tempest* emerged in the form of poetry. Percy Bysshe Shelley, Robert Browning, and W. H. Auden all have drawn inspiration from *The Tempest*. Each of these poets examines facets of the major or minor characters in the romance and imagines their responses to action within the parameters of the play itself as well as in their possible lives outside these parameters. Obviously these poets' inventions add credence to the richness and complexity of Shakespeare's characters.

In Shelley's 'With a Guitar, to Jane' (first published 1833), Ariel is allowed a dramatic monologue where he addresses Miranda and exhorts her to 'Take/This slave of Music, for the sake/Of him who is the slave of thee' (Shelley 1944: 481, lines 1–3). Ariel uses the guitar as a token to affirm his role as Miranda's 'guardian spirit' (1944: 482, line 13) and to express his longing to be a part of a human love relationship that Miranda shares with Ferdinand, but he recognises that as a part of the natural world he can only draw his harmonies and interactions from that sphere and not from the human plane. Here Ariel is presented as dutiful but melancholy in his inability to interact with Miranda, a paragon of human perfection whom he has served as 'an unseen star' (1944: 483, line 28).

Robert Browning deals with Caliban's reflections on his relationship with the island and his subjugation by Prospero in a lengthy portrait, 'Caliban Upon Setebos' (first published 1864), which expands on Caliban's speech in *The Tempest* III.ii, beginning 'Be not afeard, the isle is full of noises,/Sounds, and sweet airs, that give delight and hurt not.' The subtitle of the poem is 'Natural Theology in the Island', and as Prospero and Miranda sleep, Caliban reflects on the natural order of this tiny world, the forces that control and shape it, and his place in it. Here the reader is presented with Caliban the philosopher, not Caliban the brute, a side of him that Prospero and Miranda do not know. Browning seeks to redeem and explore Caliban's humanity.

W. H. Auden considers what life would be like for the players in Shakespeare's romance once the play has ended. 'The Sea and the Mirror' (first published 1944) is subtitled 'A Commentary on Shakespeare's *The Tempest*', and suggests that Shakespeare's play could not adequately present all of the subtext and inner life of the characters. Comprising a prologue, three main parts and a postscript, the poem starts with a statement from a stage manager to 'the critics', then moves to an address from Prospero to Ariel as Prospero prepares to leave the island, to further addresses from 'The Supporting

Cast, Sotto Voce', to a lengthy prose address from 'Caliban to the Audience'. Only in the postscript is Ariel finally allowed to address Caliban, embodying the sense of loss and lament that runs through the entire piece.

As Prospero addresses Ariel, he cannot help but feel the weight of his age, the heavy consequences of the choices made over the course of his life, and the loss, as he calls it, of his partnership with Ariel. The supporting characters begin their reflections on what has passed on the island and what awaits them back in the civilised world, with Antonio first asserting the power of his own will and his emotional separation from his brother Prospero. Antonio's isolation and alienation is noted by the other characters as a coda to their own dramatised moments of self-knowledge and self-discovery. Caliban addresses the audience as the character who will lay bare the essence of Prospero's epilogue and the entire theatrical experience. Caliban's complex and sometimes convoluted insights and assessments complicate the matters of accepting theatrical conventions like the epilogue and focusing on the essential truth of the theatrical experience:

> We must own [*for the present I speak your echo*] to a nervous perplexity not unmixed frankly, with downright resentment. How can we grant the indulgence for which in his epilogue your personified type of the creative so lamely, tamely pleaded? Imprisoned, by you, in the mood doubtful, loaded, by you, with distressing embarrassments, we are, we submit, in no position to set *anyone* free. (Auden 1968: 225)

Ariel's brief postscript is able plaintively to lay bare the emotional core of the need of the characters or actors to connect, to interact, and the ephemeral nature of that experience as Ariel speaks to Caliban:

> Weep no more but pity me,
> Fleet persistent shadow cast
> By your lameness, caught at last,
> Helplessly in love with you,
> Elegance, art, fascination,
>   Fascinated by
>   Drab mortality;
> Spare me a humiliation,
>   To your faults be true:
> I can sing as you reply
> … I
> (Auden 1968: 251)

This text is certainly one of the most challenging responses to, or adaptations of, Shakespeare's play, but it once again reveals the potential waiting to be opened up by subsequent generations of writers and readers.

In a controlled and focused fashion, students can create their own extensions of what life holds for the characters of Shakespeare's romance by imagining and writing alternative epilogues for the source text. Modelling a speech that consists of twenty lines of iambic pentameter and ten rhyming couplets, students could create the play's 'last words' for characters like Ariel, Caliban, Gonzalo and Antonio. What would they have to say about their experiences on the island, their opinion of Prospero, their plans for the future?

Connections to Modern Drama

In the late 1960s Martinique-born dramatist and poet, Aimé Césaire used Shakespeare's romance as a platform to fashion a drama to promote and explore the concepts of negritude in his play *A Tempest*. The negritude movement developed as a reaction against French imperialism in Africa and the Caribbean, and the rhetoric of the movement found its way into both cultural and literary expression. In its most basic form, negritude focused its efforts on the racist treatment of blacks by European colonists and on the affirmation of traditional African culture to prevent its decline and extinction by European customs. *The Tempest* provided Césaire and this movement with a canonical work of European 'high' culture to reveal the dehumanising effects of imperialism on both the oppressed and the oppressor.

The opening of the play draws attention to the theatrical experience as the audience watches a master of ceremonies preside over the selection of roles by a black acting company. Once roles are selected, the play follows the plot structure of the source material, but it replaces Shakespeare's poetry with vernacular speech and more contemporary poetry in the form of songs performed by Ariel, Caliban, and a new addition to the players, the African god Eshu. In Prospero's conversation with Miranda (*Temp.* I.ii), Césaire changes the reason for Prospero's presence on the island, in that his studies in Milan were focused on finding new worlds to conquer and colonise, so he is exiled for this imperialistic impulse and conveniently denounced by the Inquisition as a sorcerer to make that exile permanent. The island he inhabits is populated by two black slaves (their race is clearly defined in the cast of characters). Ariel still is the agent of Prospero's magic and Caliban grudgingly performs the menial tasks. The difference here is that Caliban tries to conspire against Prospero with Ariel before he sides with Stephano and Trinculo. In the spirit of the American civil rights movement, Caliban preaches the doctrine of violent rebellion and prefers to be called 'X', certainly an allusion to Malcolm X, while Ariel takes up the philosophy of Dr Martin Luther King and embraces a nonviolent approach. Caliban's bid for freedom complicates Prospero's machinations to marry Miranda to Ferdinand, and Prospero's attention and energies become increasingly more absorbed by his desire to dominate Caliban and quell Caliban's rhetoric of rebellion.

After the nobles are set to return to Naples, Ariel finally is granted his freedom for his good service. Ironically, Prospero confers his fatherly duties to Gonzalo and chooses to stay on the island, taking on the protection of civilisation and the salvation of Caliban as his life's work or obsession. Césaire's ending pointedly reveals that the white European Prospero eventually derives his power and misguided self-worth by forcing his political and cultural will on someone of a different race and a different ideology. He articulates this view in the following speech:

> And now, Caliban, it's you and me!
> What I have to tell you will be brief:
> Ten times, a hundred times, I've tried to save you,
> above all from yourself.
> But you have always answered me with wrath
> and venom,
> like the opossum that pulls itself up by its own tail
> the better to bite the hand that tears its from the darkness.
> Well, my boy, I shall set aside my indulgent nature
> and henceforth I will answer your violence
> with violence! (Césaire 1985: 67)

By staying on the island with Caliban, Prospero dooms himself to a struggle that only serves to dehumanise not only those he oppresses but himself as well.

In using *A Tempest* as a companion to *The Tempest*, students can obviously explore issues of imperialism and civil or human rights, as these form the basis of many ongoing and unresolved debates. A creative extension to the study of these two texts might include researching a current political or cultural struggle using the plot structure, character relationships, and themes embedded in *The Tempest* as a metaphorical structure to comment on the contemporary situation. Students could develop a proposal to illustrate how narrative could be adapted to 'update' *The Tempest* once again.

Connections to Contemporary Film

Shakespeare's *The Tempest* is no stranger to film adaptation. A highly condensed version made in Great Britain, directed by Percy Stow, premiered in 1908 and utilised imaginative sets and robust performances to replace text with broad gesticulation. During Hollywood's earliest golden age of science-fiction filmmaking in the 1950s, *The Tempest* was transported to outer space in *Forbidden Planet* (1956), where Prospero's island became an isolated planet, and his magical powers were supplanted by high-tech brain-boosting machines and the unleashed fury of the id. Over the past twenty years, the play has drawn the attention of a number of filmmakers to transport Prospero's story to other time periods, cultures, or dramatic purposes.

American filmmaker Paul Mazursky sets the action of *Tempest* on a remote island in contemporary Greece, where famed architect Philip Dimetrious has taken his daughter and his mistress to escape a mid-life crisis complicated by an adulterous wife, Antonia. The film opens with Philip on the island with Aretha, a sexually frustrated helpmate who reluctantly maintains his primitive household and Miranda, his very worldly daughter, who pines for New York nightlife. A series of flashbacks reveal how Philip becomes disillusioned with building a new casino for a gambling mogul named Alonso, why his marriage begins to disintegrate, and how he meets Aretha en route to this island refuge. On the island, Kalibanos, a shepherd and sole permanent resident, ogles Miranda, helps Philip restore a small, ancient Greek theatre, and schemes to build the island into a tourist attraction. Philip is no magician, but he implores the natural world to 'show me the magic' when he seemingly conjures up two storms: one in New York that serves to externalise his angst and anger, and a second one on the island to strand Alonso, Antonia, and their entourage and facilitate both confrontation and reconciliation. This adaptation's strength lies in effectively foregrounding its source material's theme of aging and redemption. Philip purges himself of his pride and self-absorption by leaving New York and returning to his cultural roots in Greece. There he is able to assess what he truly values as he navigates the rough waters created by a daughter who is wiser and worldlier than he imagines, and a mistress who wants him to cease his exotic globetrotting and settle into a more conventional life of suburbia and family. The film is truly a parable for what Americans refer to as the 'go go 80s', a time of greed, egoism, and competitiveness.

Shakespeare's romance appeared on American television in December 1998 under its original title and starring Peter Fonda, but this vernacular adaptation is set during the American Civil War. In this version Gideon Prosper is a plantation owner who relegates those responsibilities to his brother Anthony while Prosper learns the secrets of African conjuring from one of his black female slaves, a Mamba priestess and mother to another slave, Ariel. Prosper and his daughter Miranda seek refuge in the bayou after Prosper intervenes in the flogging of Ariel at his brother's edict, thereby incurring Anthony's wrath. The three refugees build a compound deep in the bayou with the help of Gatorman, Caliban's lecherous, stinking, complaining counterpart. Prosper is able to gain his revenge and regain his plantation when he discovers some twelve years later that Anthony is involved in leading the Union army into a trap. The most interesting aspect of this adaptation is its focus on Prosper's dabbling in African magical arts and Ariel's rejection of the occult skills that would be his cultural birthright. In this adaptation, Ariel is a tool of Prosper's magic: Prosper turns him into a bird to survey the troop manoeuvres or into an old man to lure Anthony deeper into the bayou. This version adds depth to the master–slave relationship, because although Ariel is technically freed by President Lincoln's Emancipation Proclamation, due to his great loyalty he wants Prosper to give him his freedom.

Peter Greenaway created the most controversial and spectacular adaptation of *The Tempest* in his film, *Prospero's Books*. This film uses most of Shakespeare's text but it presents that text in a very postmodern manner. In the prologue, Prospero creates a text to dramatise his need for revenge after being sent into exile. This film text is the embodiment of Prospero's famous 'Our revels now are ended' speech in Act IV. He is playwright, director, stage manager, and actor of all the major parts. The principle players, except for Ariel and the goddesses of the masque, have their lines and speeches delivered by Prospero himself (or spoken by those players off camera), and they perform their parts in an elaborate dumbshow or spectacular pantomime. The film also takes another substantial cue from Gonzalo's speech on his version of a utopian society (*Temp*. II.i). Almost every scene in the film is populated with mute, naked people who participate in the action or form a primitive human landscape, Edenic in their unconscious nakedness or, for the most part, their sensuality. This visual clash of the naked, primitive figures against the ornately clothed Milanese nobles graphically represents the two worlds in which Prospero operates and the worlds from which he must choose a future for his daughter Miranda.

The characterisations of both Ariel and Caliban are striking. Ariel is a blond curly haired cherub who is played by three different actors, alternately and simultaneously, to represent childhood, adolescence, and adulthood. Caliban is a lithe balletic dancer who physicalises his torment and desire in highly evocative movement sequences. The film draws its title from the narrative device of picturing and explaining how twenty books from Prospero's collection inform the creation of his revenge play. A voice-over narrator introduces and describes texts that range from treatises on astronomy, water, love, cosmology, and anatomy to Shakespeare's First Folio where Prospero's story ultimately finds a home. Greenaway thus reinvents Shakespeare's romance as a modern visual spectacle that forces the viewer to question the purpose of storytelling and the role of the artist in the creation of that work.

As a coda to this fertile period of adaptation of this tale, the BBC and HBO teamed with a Russian animation studio to produce a series half-hour adaptations of about half a dozen of Shakespeare's best known works, including *The Tempest*. This film in a sense reminds the scholar or teacher of the popularity of this tale as children's story or picture book. The plot has three ingredients that captivate children: danger, romance, and humour. A film adaptation of this sort provides children or reluctant older students with an entry point into the broad strokes of plot, characterisation, and theme that would be deepened with a reading or viewing experience of the original text.

The use of these free adaptations of Shakespeare's play offers the teacher a range of choices to expand students' viewing experiences. It is traditional to cap a unit of study of a play with the screening of a performance preserved as a video document such as those of the BBC series *The Shakespeare Plays*. However, the selection of one of the three cinematic adaptations described above allows students to experience the text through the lenses of both screenwriter and director. The text is no longer bound to the conventions of the stage. These adaptations help students discover how Shakespeare's work speaks to contemporary cinematic artists whose toolbox is so distinct from those of the theatrical artist.

This discussion of poetic, dramatic, and cinematic adaptations of Shakespeare's *The Tempest* is by no means definitive. For instance, there is a wealth of children's picture books that adapt the tale to younger audiences with vivid prose and illustrations. American novelist Gloria Naylor also has found inspiration from this text in her novel, *Mama Day*. The Prospero figure is a black woman living on an island in Georgia who has the power to conjure the forces of nature and exploit the powers of age-old folk practices. Then there are investigations such as that carried out by Fay Beaucamp (2001), who ponders the possibilities of Shakespeare's influences beyond travel literature and the essays of Montaigne as she compares the Akashi chapter from *The Tale of Genji* with the presence of motifs in Shakespeare's romances that are also found in Indian narratives. Obviously the study of this single text from Shakespeare's prodigious canon can and will extend scholarship and academic discourse for what seems to be 'all time' in its far-reaching influences on 19th, 20th, and certainly 21st century works.

References

Auden, W. H. (1968) 'The Sea and the Mirror', *Collected Longer Poems*, London: Faber and Faber, 199–252.

Beaucamp, Fay (2001) 'From Creation Myths to Marriage Alliances: Shakespeare's *The Tempest* and Murasaki's Akashi Chapter,' *Education About Asia* Spring, 20–25.

Browning, Robert (1956) 'Caliban upon Setebos; or Natural Theology in the Island', *Robert Browning: Selected Poetry*, New York: Holt, Rinehart and Winston, 120–28.

Césaire, Aimé (1985) *A Tempest*, trans. Richard Miller, New York: UBU.

Forbidden Planet (1956) dir. Fred McLeod Wilcox with Walter Pidgeon, Anne Francis, and Leslie Nielsen, MGM.

Naylor, Gloria (1988) *Mama Day*, New York: Vintage Contemporaries.

Prospero's Books (1991) dir. Peter Greenaway with John Gielgud, Miramax.

Shakespeare, William (1995) *The Tempest*, ed. Rex Gibson, Oakleigh, Melbourne: Cambridge University Press.

Shelley, Percy Bysshe (1944) 'With a Guitar, to Jane', *Selected Poems, Essays, and Letters*, ed. Ellsworth Barnard, New York: Odyssey Press, 481–84.

Tempest (1982) dir. Paul Mazurksy with John Cassavettes, Susan Sarandon, Molly Ringwald, and Raul Julia, Columbia Pictures.

The Tempest (1908) dir. Percy Stowe, *Silent Shakespeare* (1999) Milestone Video.

The Tempest (1992) dir. Slanislav Sokolov, Random House Video.

The Tempest (1998) dir. Jack Bender with Peter Fonda and Julian Glover, Trimark Home Video.

8

To 'See Feelingly'

READING SHAKESPEARE'S
THE RAPE OF LUCRECE

Mary Janell Metzger

Teachers rarely use Shakespeare's narrative poems. They are, after all, long, difficult to read, and they may seem a harder 'sell' than the usual plays or sonnets which, whatever you can say about them, come with some advance promotion. Yet, as I hope to demonstrate here, Shakespeare's *The Rape of Lucrece* offers students at the tertiary level a rich and provocative introduction to Shakespeare. More specifically, *The Rape of Lucrece* involves students directly in profound debates about how meaning and truth are determined, while engaging them in significant acts of historical and literary consciousness. Indeed, *The Rape of Lucrece* demands that students answer a question at the heart of their learning lives: what does it mean to take responsibility for the self in a context in which much is predetermined and yet the truth of any single answer cannot be assured?

Though *The Rape of Lucrece* has sparked some interest among critics now and then, the teaching of Shakespeare, since its commencement in the eighteenth century, has long been slanted towards tragedy and, consequently, the dilemmas of the men who figure as tragedy's protagonists. Since the late 1970s and 80s feminist critics have argued that reading and teaching such tragedies as representative of a transcendent, a-historical Shakespeare whose heroes constitute the male qua human experience does an injustice to both Shakespeare and his readers. Querying the social construction of gender roles, feminists argue, is not only useful in understanding Shakespeare's representations of men and women, but constitutes a favourite subject of his comedies and tragedies alike. Lear's and Hamlet's fear of women, like Macbeth's and Romeo's fear of becoming a woman, helps us understand the contexts in which their tragedies take shape (Garner and Sprengnether 1996). Similarly, Shakespeare's cross-dressing heroines such as Portia, Viola and Rosalind demonstrate that masculinity and femininity may be less a matter of physiology than of performing in accord with social conventions (Orgel: 1996). Yet understanding such social conventions, Shakespeare shows us, demands a highly acute consciousness wary of simplistic generalizations. What does it mean to be a 'man' or a 'woman'? Shakespeare repeatedly asks us to consider. Here in this time and place or in that? And what do such possibilities mean for the production of a good society – that is, one where justice and safety create the space for human freedom?

In his retelling of the once renowned and much debated case of the rape of Lucrece, Shakespeare takes on these issues more explicitly than in any other work. The story of Lucrece – wife and daughter of nobles serving under the tyrannous Tarquin the Proud whose rape by the King's son leads to her suicide – constituted the basis of long-standing debates in ancient, medieval and early modern societies. Her suicide is thought by some to be a valiant act of heroism: in killing herself she destroys the evidence of Tarquin's 'conquest' and constitutes the grounds for a political rebellion that culminates in the establishment of the Roman Republic – the ancestral government of England and its political offspring. She is, in this view, a model of chastity as feminine virtue par excellence. A woman whose physical beauty corresponds with her moral purity, she represents the proper object and subject that a good society creates and defends. The competing view of Lucrece argues that, in taking her own life, she is unfeminine and sinful. In her self-sacrifice, she behaves in an aggressive and prideful manner reserved for Roman men. More significantly, as Augustine first argued, she confuses her (polluted) body with her (untainted) mind, and kills what only God has the authority to destroy.

In choosing to re-present Lucrece's story there is no question that Shakespeare enters this debate. But he does so not to decide the question once and for all, as many might have, but to open that question up to his readers – that is, to create a poetic opportunity to act as judges of Tarquin and Lucrece and the acts of violence they undertake. In doing so, he offers students a rare opportunity to develop their interpretive and reasoning skills in response to an open question of grave consequence: what is the nature of truth in a world where the same oppositions between self and other, between mind and body, between reason and feeling that appear to make meaning possible also lead to violence and death?

Shakespeare frames this question first by sidelining the political context of the story in an 'Argument' that prefaces the poem itself. Much like the prologue to *Romeo and Juliet*, Shakespeare's 'Argument' lays out the complete plot of the story at the start, allowing readers to focus subsequently on *how* rather than *what* happens. In another move that suggests his interest in the social consequences of individual choice,

Shakespeare narrates the poem in the omniscient third person but situates the reader consistently and overwhelmingly inside the minds of Tarquin and Lucrece as they struggle with the effects of Tarquin's violence. Like long, extended soliloquies, these internal monologues are the primary evidence upon which we must base our judgments.

This intersection of gender psychology and literary form drew me to teach *The Rape of Lucrece* for the first time. Planning a course on gender and genre in Shakespeare, I wanted to attend to his narrative poems along with the sonnets and plays and found *The Rape of Lucrece* the most compelling of his two (*Venus and Adonis* is the other). Focused on getting the students interested in such a long and apparently demanding poem, I prepared a short introductory lecture about the historical background and psychological emphasis of the poem and prepared notes on the nature and significance of its various formal elements: Shakespeare's beginning *in media res*; his use of literary devices – apostrophes, ekphrasis, synoeciosis[1] – of mythological and literary allusion, iambic pentameter and rhyming couplets. In doing so, I functioned as many English teachers do by stressing thematic and formal aspects of the text in question. In the process, I became excited about the power of Shakespeare's treatment of the subject of rape. Like many teachers of less than contemporary texts, I consistently look for ways to connect the social and political dilemmas of Shakespeare's day to those my students face in the twenty-first century. There seemed a good chance, I thought, that the nature and consequences of rape might ignite their interest more than the seemingly distant issues of kingship, courtship or familial order at work in many of his plays.

Then, the day before we were to begin discussion of the poem, a woman was raped in broad daylight in a restroom on campus. Suddenly, the subject of rape was no longer theoretical, if it ever truly could have been, but a matter of immediate personal and collective consequence. As we settled in to begin our discussion that first day, the grief, anger and sense of mistrust generated by such violence hovered like smog around us. Despite the formal and antiquated nature of the poem's language, it no longer seemed but a literary representation of an ancient historical event. Rather, it appeared a startling instance of the power of the literary imagination to awaken a complex sense of our historicity: Shakespeare's representation of rape, the students suddenly understood, was at once far from and intimately connected with their own lives. A profound effect of this paradoxical historical consciousness was the fact that to many in the class, not least myself, the assumptions of neutrality and objectivity usually at work in our critical approaches to the poem were thrown on the table. Prepared to consider the representation of gender in the poem as an objective means of discerning its meaning, we were suddenly challenged to consider the relationship between the practical objectivism of such theories and the social commitments betrayed by our varying responses to the immediate violence of rape. Being male or female or conventionally masculine or feminine was no longer a matter for cold analysis exclusive of feeling. Indeed, the relationship between analysis as pure objectivity and social violence loomed before us like the Sphinx's riddle: we couldn't make sense of much without making sense of that.

Obviously, no one wants or needs to have the tragic events of Shakespeare's work function as a prerequisite to understanding. Yet as the Chinese wisely remind us, all crises are a form of opportunity. Reading *The Rape of Lucrece* in the wake of an on-campus rape opened our eyes to the uses of the literary imagination in the development of the social judgments and human understanding required by us as members of a community upon which we depend for both justice and safety. Who determines what rape is or means? And based on what criteria? Is rape a crime against property as its Latin roots suggest, a crime against women, or a crime against those 'feminised' as less powerful? Indeed, who decides what it means to be a man or woman? And how do these notions figure in what we conceive of as human freedom and the meaning it depends on? How, ultimately, can we reconcile our often idealistic answers to these questions with the far more complex history of human relationships? Can we begin to make judgments about the relationship between self and other that don't recreate the violent oppositions we seek to prevent? Can we, that is, combine mind and heart to 'see it feelingly', as Shakespeare's Gloucester puts it, in order to imagine a world in which rape is unthinkable?

As my brief description of our first day's discussion suggests, reading *The Rape of Lucrece* in the wake of a rape within our learning community made clear to us that resolving differing points of view about the nature of human experience and its social effects is not simply a matter of disinterested judgment. Indeed, as we were to discover, Shakespeare's poem directs us pointedly to the question of our relationship to each other and the significance of the ways in which we imagine such relationships in the stories we tell. It does this by demanding that its readers enter the longstanding debate about Lucrece – an act of interpretation (story-telling) and judgment (meaning-making) that involves difficult and significant choices. Doesn't Shakespeare's poem, some of my students demanded that first day, just reenact the violence of rape by offering us a conventionally passive, beautiful woman whose virtue can only be preserved by her death? No, no, other students wanted to insist! Shakespeare gives us something else – not a despairing Lucrece but a vengeful one! The great power of Shakespeare's poem lies in the fact that strong cases can be made for either of these views. While Lucrece's speech following the rape demonstrates her thoughtful progression from shame to rage to grief to the possibilities for obtaining justice, the narrator tells us that 'men have marble, women waxen minds/And therefore are they formed as marble will' (*ROL* 1240).[2] While divesting Lucrece of guilt for the shame of rape, the claim of 'feminine' weakness is simultaneously, Shakespeare makes clear, the ground of the shame itself.

Shakespeare points us toward this fact early in the poem in his representation of the rapist himself. In a stunning portrait of a rapist's psychology, Shakespeare allows his readers to follow Tarquin's thoughts as he moves physically and emotionally towards sexual violence. Provoked at first by envy of Collatine, Lucrece's husband, 'that meaner men should vaunt/That golden hap which their superiors want' (*ROL* 41–42), Tarquin is forced to reconcile the forms of masculine honour – physical prowess and familial continence – that sustain his sense of self with the fear and consequent rage he feels at his implied inferiority to Collatine. In the process, Tarquin offers the reader the conventional platonic account of feeling as the source of suffering and dishonour. 'O shame to knighthood and to shining arms!/O foul dishonour to my household's grave!/.../ A martial man to soft fancy's slave!' (*ROL* 197–200). Feeling, or 'fancy' in his telling is transient – 'A dream, a breath, a froth of fleeting joy' (212), a weak and insupportable because selfish pursuit set against the hierarchies of military and familial order that preserve the social good. Masculinity, and the honour it confers, is the product, Tarquin and the narrator make clear, of seeing the self in relation to other men.

Such relationships of power and the threat of subordination and annihilation they assume helped us to make sense of Shakespeare's interest in the gendered nature of shame and the consequent significance of his representation of Tarquin's vulnerability as he moves toward violence against Lucrece. As a man, Tarquin's 'surviving shame', as he calls it, is the consequence of his actions, rather than an attribute of his being. It is the residual effect and the lasting consequence of his choices that determines his relationship to others. While he tries to convince himself, and Lucrece, that secrecy will elide the issue of shame – 'Shameful it is – ay, if the fact be known' (239) – the narrator makes clear that the shame that follows upon his actions is, like his sense of self, inextricable from his relationship to other men.

Thus when Tarquin uses a perverse version of the Socratic notion that 'the good person cannot be harmed' in arguing for the rape, we were initially confused. Such self-reliance is meant to free us, my students asserted, from the transient demands of our feelings, not authorise them! The irony seems clear when, using the language of imperial conquest, Tarquin proceeds to convince himself of the justice of his violence by suggesting that in following his desire he arms himself with a form of courage motivating even the weakest of soldiers. 'Affection is my captain,' he declares, 'and he leadeth,/And when his gaudy banner is displayed,/The coward fights and will not be dismayed' (*ROL* 271–273). The meaning of the line seemed simple enough: Shakespeare reiterates the Socratic subordination of feeling to reason in offering the negative example of the rapist's choice of 'affection' rather than reason as his guide toward violence. It is feeling that gets Tarquin into trouble and if we want to avoid his mistakes ... But wait, Shakespeare says something quite different about Tarquin and the role of feeling in his act of violence in his description of Tarquin's final thought before the rape itself. Here is how he describes it:

His hand that yet remains upon her breast –
Rude ram, to batter such an ivory wall –
May feel her heart, poor citizen distressed,
Wounding itself to death, rise up and fall,
Beating her bulk, that his hand shakes withal.
This moves in him more rage and lesser pity
To make the breach and enter this sweet city.
(*ROL* 463–469)

By pointing to Tarquin's fear of human connection upon feeling Lucrece's beating heart and, further, by suggesting the psychological motive for Tarquin's crime in his consequent rage at his own 'weakness' in feeling for her, Shakespeare invites us to rethink the conventional subordination of feeling to reason in the making of social judgments. What Tarquin refuses here is not an idea of Lucrece but the shame of realising what it means to him to 'feel her heart'. As my students quickly perceived, Tarquin's rage here is the consequence of his fear of his own vulnerability, a literal and figurative impermanence captured in the image of a shaking hand.

As these lines suggest, how Shakespeare and his readers imagine the relationship between reason and feeling shapes not only how we understand the meaning of Tarquin's rape and Lucrece's later suicide, but how consequently we view the possibilities of our own human community. The politics of citizenry, Shakespeare argues here, are acted out in miniature in our response to those weaker than ourselves. Assuming that it is Tarquin's faulty rationality or his inevitable desire that lead him to rape Lucrece argues that there is in fact no possible emotional connection between Tarquin and Lucrece, and hence no alternative to the rape that doesn't rely on other forms of violent opposition. Feeling and reason in such readings are defined as opposing terms: either there is no reason which isn't in fact motivated by feeling, or the function of reason is to resist and transcend the embodied and hence transitory claims of feeling. Such arguments are regularly used by a range of readers, to clarify Shakespeare's philosophical affiliation with either humanism's transcendent celebration of 'man's' capacity and need for purely rational judgments or as illustration of his proto-postmodern grasp of the purely subjective nature of human existence. Both, however, reenact the gendered opposition of reason and feeling that is queried in the passage above.

If, however, as our class discovered, we examine the gendered nature of Tarquin's identity and its role in determining his sense of his choices, the poem suggests that the opposition between reason and feeling is less a solution to the violence at issue than its cause. In this reading, it is Tarquin's inability to locate a form of masculinity that allows his judgment access to an authorised claim of feeling that connects him to others. For Tarquin all feeling, whether lust or empathy, constitutes a challenge to his sense of identity and the self-sufficiency it requires. He rapes, Shakespeare's use of martial and imperial metaphor makes clear, not to gain something so much as to overcome something: the thought that his social value may be dependent upon the life – in this case Collatine's – of another.

Reading Shakespeare's opening representation of Tarquin in this way didn't resolve the debate about Lucrece, but it did move us to think hard about how Shakespeare chooses to represent such a controversial historical figure and how our conceptions of shame and gender roles might help us make sense of it. Certainly, in taking up the case of Lucrece, Shakespeare takes on the vexing problem of representing a woman who is at once a figure of shame and virtue. In doing so, Shakespeare cannot escape the gendered terms that constitute the story itself as well as his own historical moment: the politics of rape, suicide and revenge in ancient Rome and early modern England fix the terms of the narrative in a patriarchal logic that Aristotle puts quite succinctly:

> [I]t is both natural and expedient for the body to be ruled by the soul, and for the emotional part of our nature to be ruled by the mind, the part which possesses reason. The reverse, or even parity, would be fatal all around. This is also true as between man and other animals; for tame animals are by nature better than wild, and it is better for them all to be ruled by men, as it secures their safety. Again, as between male and female the former is by nature, superior and ruler, the latter inferior and subject. And this must hold good of mankind in general. (1992 *1254b2*)

The hierarchical binary articulated here, in which women, nature, the body and its feelings, are subordinated to men, civilization and reason, is echoed in Shakespeare's poem by the narrator and Lucrece herself. Her violated body is 'polluted', 'corrupted', and even in death, 'Some of her blood still pure and red remained/And some looked black, and that false tarquin-stained' (*ROL* 1742–43). Unlike Tarquin, Lucrece bears the shame of Tarquin's violence in her body for it is in her body – as a 'good' woman – that her virtue lies. Confronting the historical consciousness of gender at work in the poem raised profound questions for my students about how any individual escapes the cultural conventions of their own historical moment to make meanings that resist oppression and violence – especially when such meanings constitute the unquestioned values of one's community.

The trouble, Shakespeare makes clear in his depiction of Lucrece, is that all 'truths' are compounds made up of experience, knowledge, belief, desire and possibility. It is no surprise then to find the pre-rape Lucrece is a kind of masculine fantasy of female as commodity. Her existence, as Shakespeare tells us in the 'Argument', is defined by waiting, yet a waiting that is less process than object. In a game the men devise to test their wives' virtue, the wives of the other Roman soldiers are 'all found dancing, and revelling, or in several disports' when their husbands return unexpectedly. Lucrece, however, is engaged in the act of 'spinning amongst her maids'. As handbooks of the period explain, while productive of a certain domestic product, handwork in the case of noblewomen was aimed at prohibiting rather than generating female activity and the forms of existence associated with it. John Taylor offers the following recommendation for English women in 1631: 'It will increase their peace, enlarge their store,/To use their tongues less and their needles more' (Aughterson 1995: 211).

Historicising Lucrece's feminine virtue with a look at what the injunction against idleness meant for women in Shakespeare's time helped us see the profound difference between the virtuous pre-rape Lucrece and the problematic-because-violent post-rape Lucrece that Shakespeare, following the historical sources closely, offers us. One of the most significant aspects of Shakespeare's poem is how much 'tongue' Lucrece is allowed after the rape. Indeed, there is no way to make sense of the poem without reconciling the early Lucrece, who lives to wait upon the desires of others and the later figure, whose speech queries in voluminous and pointed form the nature of her own existence. By historicising ancient and early modern notions of gender with the help of Aristotle and Taylor, it was not hard for the students to recall the connections between Aristotle's subordinated categories – the body, feeling, women, wilderness – and the fear of social impropriety and disorder such connections implied. Such impropriety entails, Aristotle's argument for social good makes clear, individual shame – the sense, to put it simply, of being inadequate to one's community.

Asking ourselves what the connection is and should be between body, feeling, voice and community, we began to understand a distinction between guilt and shame that writer Nancy Mairs explains in describing the shame entailed by her rebellious disabled body. 'I feel guilt or embarrassment for something I've done; shame for who I am. I may stop doing bad or stupid things, but I can't stop being. How can I help but be ashamed?' Speech, Mairs argues, constitutes a crucial form of resistance to such objectification in its assumption of community. '[S]peaking out loud is an antidote to shame,' Mairs claims. 'I can subvert its power by acknowledging who I am, shame and all, and in doing so, raising what was hidden, dark and secret about my life into the plain light of shared experience' (Mairs 1994: 276–77).

Such 'speaking out loud' is what Shakespeare allows Lucrece to do. What Shakespeare represents in Lucrece's post-rape discourse, students discover, is a struggle to imagine the self beyond the hierarchies of value that predicate the rape itself – powerful, powerless – as well the assumed options – to live in shame or die in sin – that follow from it. It's important to note that the early Lucrece of the poem is conveyed to us through the voices of others, Tarquin and the narrator, and that we only hear from her directly when she is threatened with violence. Suddenly bereft of the physical safety which her status as the wife of Collatine and the daughter of Lucius have provided,

Shakespeare suggests that she must now negotiate her relationship to Tarquin and later her husband and family without benefit of men's surety. Perhaps most importantly, the Lucrece of the Argument and early portion of the poem is incapable of imagining other women unlike herself whose 'shame' guarantees the value of her 'virtue'. While she fails to convince herself in the end of the possibility of another kind of life than the one she's lost, her speech marks a space between her despair in it and the terms that produced it, and another kind of existence in which feeling and the human connection it assumes is sustainable.

In her apostrophe to Night and Time, in the ekphrasis, and in her final speech to her father and husband, Lucrece explores the nature of the shame both imposed on and experienced by her as a consequence of the acts of another. Throughout her speech, Lucrece seeks to tie her feelings to her commitments to others. By 'speaking out loud', as Mairs would say, Lucrece defies the injunction to silence literally made by Tarquin and figuratively imposed on all women as objects of shame. Unlike Tarquin's speech, Lucrece's aims at constructing a world in which her feeling can inform her judgment and thus reconstruct the sense of social identity the rape has undermined. Thus the significance of her reading of other feminine figures of suffering, such as Philomel and Hecuba, lies not in her failure to find in them examples of heroic action, but in the sense of shared feeling they provide in her struggle to reconstruct a world in which her commitments to others do not conclude in violence but in community (*ROL* 1128–48; 1443–70).

In doing so, Lucrece offers a significant model of reading in the pursuit of justice, reading as an act of constructing the social subject, whose virtue is not decided in opposition or abstraction but by relation to others like and unlike herself. The feelings she expresses – grief, rage, empathy, hate, and pity among others – help her negotiate between abstract arguments about ideal human existence and the fact that the meaning of her life must be sought and finally found in her relationship to others. Lucrece's suicide in this reading is neither the mark of her 'quasi-masculine' heroism nor the sign of absolute feminine passivity. While an act of violence against herself, her suicide constitutes an act of despair in the possibility of living in a world where terror of feeling results in the violence of her immutable shame and Tarquin's rape. Like all subjects, Shakespeare's poem suggests, Lucrece's judgment, like our own, is and should be shaped by feeling for others. To be completely objective, or as she puts it, to have 'true eyes'(*ROL* 748), is not, she makes clear, to be a subject at all and consequently, unable to judge the justice of any act, including her own. In hundreds of lines and the better part of the poem, Lucrece explores exactly what her shame means in a culture in which women's identities are dependent on their status as sexual property. As Catherine Belsey explains, Lucrece's grief, like rape itself, 'call[s] into question the distinction taken for granted by so many modern readers between mind and the organism of which it is a part' (2002: 331). The violence done to Lucrece is neither solely to her body nor her psyche. Given that inescapable fact, her conclusion that the dramatic staging of her victim status via suicide offers the best possibility of justice is much harder to judge as a failure of objectivity. The meaning of human freedom for lives punctuated by death and shaped by inescapable social practices seems suddenly less a matter of self-sufficiency guaranteed by absolute truths and more an opportunity to join our hearts and minds in speaking against the shame that brings both Tarquin and Lucrece to seek the recourse of violence.

Indeed, while reading a poem about rape makes consideration of social context inevitable, the traditional practice of the English classroom inclines toward a formalism that makes the expression of feeling entailed by such considerations often difficult. In my class's case, the distance usually provided by academic consideration of such historical and social events was destroyed by our recent experience of the very violence at issue in the poem. Yet, as English teachers often remind their students, to read from one's particular social commitments remains dangerous: be careful, we advise, remain objective! Avoid the word 'I' or use it sparingly! The reasons for such practical objectivism are clear when faced with any piece of writing in which the 'I' dominates everything else. Yet as I began to realize in teaching *The Rape of Lucrece*, understanding Shakespeare's representation of Tarquin and Lucrece and hence the nature of rape itself forces us to recognize the crucial role of feeling in all social judgments – not least those we make in judgment of other's stories.

The ambiguity at work in *The Rape of Lucrece* – as narrative poetry and as history – makes any recourse to pure facts impossible. What facts we know – that Tarquin raped Lucrece, that Lucrece committed suicide, that rape is shame-full – do not, Shakespeare makes clear, lead to any guaranteed truth in judgment. What answers readers of Shakespeare's poem come to about Tarquin, Lucrece, the causes and thus the meaning of their violence, and the possibility of justice in such a world, can be girded only by the force of each student's heartfelt reasoning and the clarity of his or her own commitments. In doing so, students discover the power of the human voice – Shakespeare's and their own – to join heart and mind in the creation of community and the possibilities for meaning and freedom it suggests. Teaching Shakespeare, *The Rape of Lucrece*, reminds us, should be an exercise in discovering the power of the human voice, never a matter of simply documenting it.

Notes

1   Apostrophe: sudden exclamatory address; an exclamatory passage addressed to a particular person (frequently absent or dead) or thing. Ekphrasis: (ecphrasis) a lucid self-contained explanation or description. Synoeciosis: A coupling or bringing together of contraries,

but not in order to oppose them to one another. See Hussey (1992) for an introduction to Shakespeare's rhetoric; see Harmon and Holman (2000) for definitions of these and other literary and rhetorical devices used in the works of Shakespeare.

2 Citations from *The Rape of Lucrece* are given as *ROL* followed by line number(s), according to the edition listed under Shakespeare in the References.

References

Aristotle (1992) *The Politics*, Translated by T.A. Sinclair. Revised Edition. London: Penguin Books.

Belsey, C. (2001) 'Tarquin Dispossessed: Expropriation and Consent in *The Rape of Lucrece*.' *Shakespeare Quarterly 52*, 315–35.

Garner, S. N. and M. Sprengnether (1996) *Shakespearean Tragedy and Gender*, Bloomington: Indiana University Press.

Harmon, William and C. Hugh Holman. (2000) *A Handbook To Literature*. Eighth Edition. Upper Saddle River, New Jersey: Prentice Hall.

Hussey, S. S. (1992) *The Literary Language of Shakespeare*. Second Edition. London: Longman, 65–90.

Mairs, N. (1994) 'Carnal Acts' in P. Foster (ed) *Minding the Body* New York: Anchor Books, 267–82.

Orgel, S. (1996) *Impersonations: The Performance of Gender in Shakespeare's England*, Cambridge: Cambridge University Press.

Taylor, John (1995) 'The Needle's Excellency' in K. Aughterson (ed) *Renaissance Woman: A Sourcebook*, London: Routledge, 210–12.

Shakespeare, William (1997) 'The Rape of Lucrece', *The Norton Shakespeare*, ed. Stephen Greenblatt, et al. New York: W.W. Norton & Company.

9

2002, A Shakespearean Odyssey

POSTCOLONIAL THEORY AND PEDAGOGY FROM THE METROPOLIS TO THE MARGINS

Paromita Chakravarti and Swati Ganguly

At a curriculum revision meeting of the English Department convened in August 2001 at Visva-Bharati University, Santiniketan, India, a member of the faculty suggested that there was perhaps an imbalance in the existing postgraduate syllabus which had an entire paper devoted to Shakespeare. This privileging of Shakespeare seemed to be unacceptable, especially in light of the fact that other more 'relevant' topics like post-colonial studies could not be accommodated within the mandatory eight papers prescribed by the University Grants Commission for the postgraduate course.[1] The suggestion of removing some of the prescribed Shakespearean plays to accommodate postcolonial literature and theory was met with alarm. Giving Shakespeare such short shrift was considered an act of sacrilege. There was also considerable resistance to the idea of introducing postcolonial studies as a compulsory paper, because its close align-ment with the disciplines of history and politics seemed to locate it outside the domain of 'pure' literature. It was further argued that postcolonial studies would alienate the average student who would not be able to access its theoretical complexity and sophistication. Shakespeare's work, notwithstanding the demands it made on the linguistic ability of the student, was considered more accessible.

The pitting of Shakespeare and postcolonial studies against one another in a race for survival exemplifies the crisis in contemporary Indian academia. On the one hand Shakespeare is identified as colonial baggage and most English departments now feel a moral obligation to perform a 'postcolonial act' of eliminating the Bard from their syllabi. On the other hand, Shakespeare, deemed the best gift of English education, familiarised through two hundred years of colonialism, is for many Indians, 'one of us, a brother under the skin' (Ray 2000: 17), and so more accessible than postcolonial studies which seems to be a new-fangled and unfamiliar product, both alien and alienating. In this paper we propose to investigate the politics of pedagogy which posits Shakespeare and postcolonial studies as oppositional and exclusive categories, and show how the project of 'teaching Shakespeare postcolonially' can provide a radical and viable alternative that may solve this seeming impasse.

Shakespeare versus Postcolonial

The identification of Shakespeare as the colonial bogey has to be understood in the historical context of the introduction of English Studies in India in 1835. The dissemination of English language and literature was the tool chosen by the British administration to create a native elite educated in Western ideas and values who would need to be co-opted if the empire was to be consolidated (Vishwanathan 1989; Bagchi 1991; Singh 1996). As the supreme exemplar of European humanistic ideals, Shakespeare became the cornerstone of the English syllabi in schools and colleges. In pedagogy and performance Shakespeare plays were chosen as the conduit for diffusing Enlightenment ideals of reason, liberalism, progressivism and modernity embodying the highest 'human' values which transcended cultural differences.

These universalist assumptions about 'human nature' which underlie liberal humanist Shakespeare pedagogy posed a certain danger. Obliterating disparities between coloniser and colonised created a false belief among the Indian elite that they were in fact closer to their European masters than their fellow countrymen.[2] But these assumptions were also empowering in so far as they offered a certain class of Indians a foothold in the coloniser's culture, thus allowing the Indian to emerge from the confines of a traditional, caste-ridden society and acquire the confidence of belonging to a larger, 'modern', secular community. Thus Shakespeare was not just foisted on the natives as a means of hegemonic control; his work had a certain liberating and modernising potential, then as even now, in independent India.

Shakespeare is entrenched in our psyches and educational systems with an obduracy that cannot simply be wished away. He represents the social aspirations and dreams of a beleaguered middle-class for whom an English degree still confers respectability and provides greater social and economic currency in the marriage and job markets. The potency of Shakespeare in our collective consciousness and his metonymic function as the embodiment of traditional English studies make him the obvious target of attack from postcolonial theorists who wish to decolonise the discipline. But attempts to do so create a genuine sense of dispossession and arouse fears of being marginalised from the mainstream western culture among a large section of Indian academics.

Desperate justifications are provided to prove the continuing relevance of

Shakespeare in Indian lives. In his inaugural address at the World Shakespeare Conference, 2000, held in Calcutta, the President of the Shakespeare Society of Eastern India proudly proclaimed that 'Shakespeare is more relevant to us, has more meaning for us Indians', and went so far as to suggest that Shakespeare should be taught as an 'Indian writer' (Ray 2000: 17). Tracing parallels between medieval, feudal England and twentieth-century India, he tried to prove that incidents of witch hunting and the persistence of the extended family system in India make *Macbeth* and *King Lear* more relevant to the Indian student than his/her European/American counterpart living in an advanced society divorced from the Shakespearean context. Interestingly, this address was promoted as a bold postcolonial reading of Shakespeare. This rather skewed and shrill special pleading on behalf of the peculiar relevance of Shakespeare to Indian situations is the last-ditch endeavour of a besieged Shakespearean who senses his occupation nearly gone and tries to reclaim his territory seemingly usurped by the Postcolonial brigade. By claiming this completely historical appropriation and indigenisation of Shakespeare to be a form of postcolonial reading, the speaker overturns the ideological foundations of postcolonial theory on the one hand, and on the other, he appropriates its privileged position.

For most scholars and teachers working in India, postcolonial theory remains a foreign and rather incomprehensible enemy which threatens to destabilise the comforts of traditional English literary studies but must be appeased. For them, postcolonial theorists appear to engage in a polemic that seems opposed to the aesthetics of a liberal humanist literary culture, and who seem to speak in an obfuscatory rhetoric, in books that most Indians cannot afford.

Indeed postcolonial theory is largely generated under the aegis of the Anglo-American academies and for the consumption of the West. Critics have noted this western endorsement of a certain kind of cultural politics as the defining quality of the postcolonial. Arif Dirlik fixes the originary point of the postcolonial as the moment 'When Third world intellectuals have arrived in the First World academe' (Dirlek 1994: 328). Anthony Kwame Appiah describes postcoloniality as

> the condition of what we might ungenerously call the comprador intelligentsia: a relatively small group of writers and thinkers who mediate the trade in cultural commodities of world capitalism at the periphery. (Brydon 2000: 93)

It is these highly visible, highly regarded Third World intellectuals working in metropolitan academies who formulate our postcoloniality for us in a manner which many of us find unsuitable, even counterproductive. Much as they have radically challenged and revolutionised the discipline of English studies, the fruits of their endeavours remain inaccessible for most students in India who would much rather have their Shakespeare and their Bradley. While we recognise the need to question the status quo, we would also like to urge that postcolonial studies, particularly theory, cannot be imposed from above – it must first be properly disseminated and assimilated before it can even begin to address the issues of the complex cultural investments in Shakespeare in India. Postcolonial studies should not dislodge Shakespeare but bring Shakespeare into its ambit to transform both Shakespearean pedagogy and postcolonial theory in original and profitable ways.

Postcolonial Shakespeare versus reading Shakespeare postcolonially

Postcolonial readings of Shakespeare became popular in western academia in the 80s. Inspired by New Historicism and its interest in marginal histories, the early postcolonial interpretations focussed on questions of race and cultural otherness in Shakespeare's plays.[3] Through these issues postcolonial critics attempted to destabilise the centrality of the Shakespearean text, challenge the way in which the relationship of the text and context was traditionally construed, examine how Shakespeare was deployed as a colonising instrument and address the politics of reception of Shakespeare in climes not his own. But unfortunately, the ideological underpinnings of postcolonial Shakespeare criticism remained for the most part unexplored in the way that it was disseminated and popularised.

For most English literature students in India, postcolonial Shakespeare means little more than evincing a superficial interest in the Moor, Shylock, Aaron, Caliban or the changeling 'Indian' child. Thus only specific Shakespearean texts are thought to lend themselves to postcolonial readings because of their obvious engagement with 'colonial' issues of racial and cultural otherness. *The Tempest* and *Othello* have received this status of the most favoured texts seized upon by Shakespeareans anxious to jump on the postcolonial bandwagon. But this project has remained severely limited and has failed to address the rest of the Shakespeare corpus which continues to be taught in traditional New Criticism modes.

Even in the teaching of *Othello* and *The Tempest*, there has been no radical questioning of the liberal humanist aesthetics which underlie our teaching practices. The occasional references to racial othering and colonisation within a pedagogy which remains unchanged in its ideology and methodology are merely token self-congratulatory gestures of having arrived on the postcolonial scene. Resistance to what is understood as the 'anti-literary' political agenda of postcolonial theory continues unabated even as cosmetic concessions are made to accommodate it.

This understanding of the political and the literary as mutually exclusive categories was foregrounded in the experience of a young and enthusiastic colleague who lamented that his attempts at a radical postcolonial reading of Shakespeare in class was met with indignation on grounds that he was violating the pleasure principle (the *sahitya rasa*) which is the function and aim of literature. In the students' perception (which echoes the traditional view of a pure and universal 'literary' aesthetic) the pleasures of the text are located in a neutral space free from the contamination of politics and history. They refuse to consider that our notions of the 'literary' as 'pure' and of Shakespeare as a transcendent signifier of the values of universal, transcultural, apolitical 'literariness' are ideologically constructed. Perhaps the only way to address this politics of the aesthetic is to create an aesthetic of politics.

This might be achieved by laying bare the ideological premises of Shakespeare studies in colonial and postcolonial India and by ensuring that this awareness of the political positioning of Shakespeare vis-a-vis the Indian student should become an integral part of Shakespearean pedagogy in our classrooms. It should no longer be possible to teach Shakespeare in an unmediated, a-historical fashion. The historical specificity of the students' postcolonial subjectivity and identity should be stressed as the first step in understanding his/her relationship to any Shakespearean text. Teachers should be encouraged to historicise Shakespeare, not only as an early modern English writer, but as a vehicle of cultural colonisation in nineteenth-century India. Shakespearean plays should not be taught in a historical vacuum, as if teaching them in India and Britain were the same. At the same time care should be taken to ensure that Shakespeare does not get indigenised in such a way that he becomes 'an Indian writer', as claimed by the President of the Shakespeare Society of Eastern India.

Our pedagogy should treat Shakespeare as both ours and the coloniser's, emphasising our distance from this sixteenth-century English writer while acknowledging our own undeniable and long familiarity with him. This can be done not so much through deploying postcolonial theory, but more through unearthing the history of our relationship with Shakespeare and making it available to the student as an intrinsic part of his/her own experience of any particular Shakespearean text. This would release us from the constricted and reductive notion of token 'postcolonial Shakespearean texts' (like *The Tempest* and *Othello*) and make it possible to read all Shakespearean texts postcolonially. Teaching Shakespeare postcolonially would involve familiarising students with the history of the dissemination, pedagogy and performance of Shakespearean plays in India and tracing the story of the formation of the Shakespearean canon in our syllabi. Accounts of indigenous adaptations, translations and performances can provide interesting insights into the way in which Shakespeare became a means through which colonial modernity was both appropriated and occasionally resisted.

As we envisage it, this would necessitate evolving a methodology in which a series of introductory lectures would be provided to the students, familiarising them with the tradition of Shakespeare culture in colonial and postcolonial India. We would like to suggest some possible sources which could help the teacher in this field: Jasodhara Bagchi's 'Shakespeare in Loin Cloths: English Literature and the Early

Nationalist Consciousness' (1991), the Introduction to Loomba and Orkin (1998), Jyotsna Singh's 'Shakespeare and the "civilising mission"' (1996), and Harish Trivedi's 'Shakespeare in India: Colonial contexts' (1995). This is by no means an exhaustive list, and of course it will be necessary to keep updating it with new scholarship, which in turn would ensure a continuous traffic between postcolonial pedagogy and research that we feel is sadly lacking in most universities.

Equally important is the project of building an archive of indigenous critical responses to Shakespeare and compiling checklists of translations and adaptations as well as documenting how Shakespeare's plays permeated the popular consciousness through vernacular film and media. This will provide the apparatus through which students may access the reservoir of community memory and consciously resist the act of collective amnesia on which the edifice of essentialist Shakespearean studies was built in the colonies. It would also help in the demystification and dismantling of a liberal, apolitical aesthetic based on the suppression of the ideological underpinnings of the Shakespearean text and gradually lead us towards an aesthetic of politics in which the pleasure of reading will not be dependent on any essentialist notion of 'authentic literary value'. Ultimately, such an enterprise would not be limited to Shakespeare teaching only but will provide a tool for a radical revamping of the discipline of English studies as a whole and make it an integral part of Culture Studies.

However, it is pointless to talk about methodological and ideological reform without addressing the material conditions which keep the orthodox teaching practices in place – like the production and marketing of the various 'notebooks' which are actually mugbooks designed to help the student pass examinations. These notebooks comprise corrupt versions of texts with rather dubious paraphrases and annotations. The popularity and success of these notebooks lie in their affordability (they are significantly cheaper than foreign editions such as Arden, New Cambridge or Oxford) and their ability to provide ready-made answers which use the language of traditional humanist readings of Shakespeare in an adulterated form. Since this vocabulary of affect has been internalised by students as the true expression of 'literary sensibility' they find it easy to memorise and regurgitate this language in examinations. Any attempt to change existing Shakespeare teaching methods flounders in the face of the complex nexus of a 'notebook culture': predictable question patterns in examinations supported by a syllabus that continues unchanged for years.

So the project of making Shakespeare more meaningful to the postcolonial situation will have to provide inexpensive textbooks which would put the students' transactions with the Shakespearean text into a historical perspective. This would give them an understanding of their unique position as postcolonial readers of Shakespeare and provide them with a confidence in the legitimacy of such a position. Instead of seeking to speak in the borrowed voices of dead white male critics supplied by the notebooks, the Indian student would be encouraged to find his/her own niche in the Shakespearean edifice. Such textbooks will create for students a notion of their own agency in the pedagogic system and foster a sense of empowerment by connecting Shakespeare to their lives.

Methodology and Location: A Tale of Two Universities

The project of reading Shakespeare postcolonially must take into account the historical specificity of the pedagogical situations of different universities in different parts of India. It is not feasible, indeed not even desirable to adopt a homogenised prescriptive course of postcolonial Shakespeare for all Indian universities. Yet, we hope to show through our discussion of Shakespeare teaching practices in the two universities of Jadavpur and Visva-Bharati, how the project of teaching Shakespeare postcolonially can prove to be flexible enough to serve the very different needs of students from varied socio-cultural backgrounds in meaningful ways. It can encourage privileged students who have access to metropolitan postcolonial theory to question its suitability to their specific historical situations and apply it appropriately to their reading of Shakespeare in an informed way. Those who are neither linguistically competent nor affluent enough to afford a familiarity with theory would find in our methodology an approach to Shakespeare which takes their particular postcolonial location into account and provides them a medium through which both theory and Shakespeare can become accessible. Our project can revitalise both Shakespeare and postcolonial studies at Jadavpur and Visva-Bharati, bridging the divide between urban and suburban institutions, between middle-class and underprivileged students, and between Shakespeare and theory, ensuring some degree of parity of access to a cultural capital (represented by both Shakespeare and postcolonial studies) jealously guarded by the elite, whether of a orthodox/colonial or of a progressive/postcolonial persuasion.

Jadavpur University was originally established in Calcutta, the erstwhile capital of the British empire, as part of the anti-colonial nationalist endeavour to develop an alternative to the highly anglicised and elitist centres of traditional humanist education like the Presidency College. After independence, its radical character was retained in its involvement in leftist politics, women's movements and in its ability to provide a hospitable environment for underprivileged students from suburbia. The Department of English fostered an anti-essentialist critical stance and sensitised students to questions of class, gender and race.

However, the character of the Department changed towards the end of the 80s, with government endorsement of a certain kind of alternative politics and a change in the class composition of the student body. Falling standards in Presidency College because of over-bureaucratisation and poor administrative policies witnessed an exodus of students and teachers to Jadavpur University. The majority were from upper-middle-class backgrounds with education in expensive schools where the medium of instruction is English. In the process of this bourgeoisification of the English Department, its radicalism was coopted by the traditional elite to produce a new seat of power and prestige for English Studies.

With the generous grants provided by the University Grants Commission and with a star-studded, western-educated teaching faculty, students at Jadavpur now have easy access to the knowledge and power of the international academy. They are part of the Anglo-American conference networks and are familiar with the latest and most expensive books on theory, which locate them in a privileged space. With their gaze fixed on Ivy League colleges, they quickly realise that engaging in postcolonial studies gives them a certain edge in the international scholarship market where mainstream subjects like Shakespeare studies seem unfashionable. These students regard the traditional elements in their syllabus as a burden they can do without. This view stems from a severely limited understanding of postcolonial theory as applicable to only certain kinds of texts produced under colonial or postcolonial conditions. It is largely ignorance about the potency of Shakespeare in our collective imagination that allows many of these highly competent Jadavpur students to dismiss the Bard with such ease.

Texts which outline the history of India's varied and persistent engagement with and investment in Shakespeare would help students to realise why his plays still continue to be taught. They would provide ways of using postcolonial theory and colonial history to read those authors whom they consider dispensable reminders of our colonial past. Such texts would also help them to appreciate their specific historical location vis-a-vis Shakespeare and to negotiate with that location, instead of having it defined by the postcolonial theorists in the West who can afford to cry for Shakespeare's blood, without considering the reality of how and why he continues to be important in our lives and syllabi, particularly in the less privileged English departments of Indian universities.

By contrast, the Department of English and Other Modern European Languages at Visva-Bharati, Santiniketan, can hardly boast of a teacher and student community comparable to Jadavpur. Here, Shakespeare commands not only interest but becomes the focus of debates which question the very foundations of the postcolonial subject's relationship to the discipline of English as it is taught in contemporary India. The implications of this phenomenon can only be understood in the context of the history and current pedagogical realities of the institution.

Located in a small town about three hundred kilometres from the metropolis of Calcutta, Visva-Bharati is an institution established by Rabindranath Tagore in the 1920s with an anti-imperialist bias and a vision of academic and cultural excellence. The aspiration with which Tagore set up Visva-Bharati as an avant-garde seat of learning has become a distant dream.

For all practical purposes the university caters to students of the adjoining small town and nearby industrial townships. A large section of them come from under-privileged families and many of them are probably first generation learners, handicapped by a lack of basic English comprehension and writing skills. It might therefore seem a foregone conclusion that these students would be daunted by the prospect of reading Shakespeare and would invariably depend on 'notebooks' to see them through exami-nations. Though this may be true of a large number of students, there are exceptions for whom Shakespeare has become a means of empowerment for engaging meaning-fully with the issue of their postcolonial subjectivity and identity. Postcoloniality for this handful of interested young people has not arrived via the 'newfangled' postcolonial theory but through accessing the history of Shakespeare reception/appropriation in Bengal/India.

In recent years two students of the Department of English have begun research into the complex ways in which late 19th and early 20th century middle-class Indians responded to Shakespeare in the areas of pedagogy and performance. For one of them the 'rediscovery' of Shakespeare occurred when he read an essay by Tagore entitled 'Shakuntala', written in 1907, which compares a Sanskrit play, *Abhijnanasakuntalam*, by the 5th century poet-dramatist Kalidasa, with Shakespeare's *The Tempest*. Kalidasa had in a sense been rediscovered for the 19th century Bengali audience through the Orientalist enterprise of William Jones, whose translation of the play *Sacontala* sparked off the interest in classical Sanskrit drama. Not only was Kalidasa referred to as the Shakespeare of India but as Trivedi notes, 'the general strategy of pitting the best of English literature, Shakespeare, against the best of native Sanskrit literature gradually developed into a recognised nationalist response' (1995: 18). However, instead of the beaten track of the 'head on point-by-point contrast' (1995: 18) between Kalidasa and Shakespeare, Tagore provides a rare insight into *The Tempest* as a study of power and domination. He writes:

> In *The Tempest* Man does not exist in a beneficial and affectionate relationship with his envi-ronment – he wishes to diminish and dominate others. It is in fact a play about power con-flicts. Having had to abandon his kingdom, Prospero uses his magic to subdue the realm of nature. The few shipwrecked survivors conspire, betray and attempt to kill each other for the domination of the empty island. At the close of the play there is a resolution but not an end to this evil. Fear, repression and absence of opportunity keeps demonic nature temporarily suspended, in sullen abeyance like Caliban, but the poison in its tooth and claw remains. (Tagore, 1940: 529. Translated from the original Bengali by the authors)

At a time when *The Tempest* was read as an epitome of a pastoral romance, Tagore's ability to demystify the ideology of Prospero's magic as a political enterprise may be regarded as truly radical. Since students identify such critiques either in terms of New Historicist or Postcolonialist concerns, it came as a revelation to this student that it was possible to locate a proto-postcolonial Shakespeare in the forgotten or neglected vernacular criticism of colonial Bengal. Shakespeare, even political and alternative Shakespeare, could now be freed from the hegemony of western discourses and radicalised along a new axis. This possibility gave the student the confidence of assuming a more active role in a pedagogic system which had previously seemed only to impose unfamiliar ideas on him. For him, a first generation learner from an economically depressed section of the agrarian community, reading Shakespeare post-colonially became an enabling tool.

It is evident that our methodology would allow these students to acquire a foothold in the terrain of postcolonial studies which still appears alien to them and would also bring Shakespeare closer to their lives, mediated through the history of continued indigenous negotiations. Thus teaching Shakespeare postcolonially can address different needs of different student groups to make Shakespeare more relevant to their specific postcolonial locations.

It would be easy to do away with Shakespeare as a colonial bogey, but this could represent an opting out of history, a turning away from real issues, a preferring of an abstract theoretical simplification over the complexity of our lived postcoloniality. In this context we would like to evoke Trivedi's Hindi term for Postcolonialism, *uttarupaniveshvad* (1997: 43), to describe our understanding of what this postcoloniality means to us. The word contains within it the notion of an active dialogue (the Sanskrit prefix *uttar* means both 'after' and 'an answer and opposition to' colonialism or *upaniveshvad*) with colonialism and its legacies. Unlike 'Postcolonialism', it is not a passive or a neutral term, and stresses our locational and temporal specificity as a postcolonial nation, as well as implying resistance to the neocolonial domination that exists in the western attempt to fix a postcolonial identity on once-colonised nations. Through our attempts to devise a Shakespeare-*uttarupaniveshvad*, we have tried to provide an inroad into why and how Shakespeare must become a lived question in postcolonial India.

Notes

1   The University Grants Commission is the governmental body which oversees higher education in India. 'Paper' here follows British academic usage in meaning a single, usually semester-length, course.

2   Ania Loomba (1989: 21) describes this new English education as offering a 'programme of building a new man who would feel himself a citizen of the world while the very face of the world was being constructed in the mirror of the dominant culture of the West'.

3   For a history of the development of postcolonial criticism of Shakespeare see the Introduction
    to Loomba and Orkin (1998).

References

Appiah, A. (1991) 'Is the post- in postmodernism the post- in postcolonial?', *Critical Inquiry* 17,
    336–57. Reprinted in Brydon, D (2000) ed. *Postcolonialism: Critical Concepts in literary and
    cultural studies* vol. 1, London: Routledge, 85–104.

Bagchi, J. (1991) 'Shakespeare in Loin Cloths: English Literature and Early Nationalist
    Consciousness in Bengal', Joshi, S. ed. *Rethinking English: Essays in Literature, Language,
    History*, New Delhi: Trianka, 146–159.

Dirlek, A. (1994) 'The Postcolonial Aura: Third World Criticism in the Age of Global
    Capitalism', *Critical Inquiry* 20, 328–56.

Loomba, A. (1989) *Gender, Race, Renaissance Drama*, Manchester: Manchester University Press.

Loomba, A. and Orkin, M. (1998) ed. Introduction, *Post-Colonial Shakespeares*, London:
    Routledge, 1–19.

Ray, Amitava, 'Indianizing and Contemporanizing Shakespeare', *Colonial and Postcolonial
    Shakespeares: Papers and Proceedings of the World Shakespeare Conference*, Calcutta, 16–28.

Singh, J. (1996) 'Shakespeare and the "civilising mission"', *Colonial Narratives/Cultural Dialogues*,
    London: Routledge, 120–152.

Vishwanathan, G. (1989) *Masks of Conquest: Literary Study and British rule in India*, London:
    Faber and Faber.

Tagore, R.(1940) *Rabindra Rachanabali* (The Complete Works of Tagore), vol. V, Calcutta:
    Vishwabharati Press, 521–537.

Trivedi, H. (1995) 'Shakespeare in India: Colonial contexts', *Colonial Transactions*, Manchester:
    Manchester University Press, 10–28.

Trivedi, H. (1997) 'India and Postcolonial Discourse', Prafulla C. Kar ed. *Critical Theory: Western
    and Indian*, Delhi: Pencraft International, 36–55.

10

Teaching and Risk

DOING AND UNDOING SHAKESPEARE

D. Kay Johnston and Margaret Maurer

'What is *pourquoi*, do or not do?' (*Twelfth Night*, I.iii.98)

Pourquoi, of course, is 'why,' and it is always a question to be asked about curriculum: as, for example, why teach Shakespeare's plays? Asking why a thing is to be done is, however, as Sir Andrew Aguecheek in *Twelfth Night* intuits (though his insight sounds accidental), a form of questioning whether something ought to be done at all. The answer we want to put forward here is yes, it should be done; and we want to propose a reason why: teaching Shakespeare's plays creates a place in the curriculum where students and teachers can take risks together, that is, where teachers can undertake with students an examination of texts that provocatively resist attempts to impose a coherent interpretation on them.

This may seem a counterintuitive thing to say about Shakespeare, whose status as a writer has, since the eighteenth century anyway, been assured by the consensus that his work is timelessly meaningful. At the point of designing curriculum, that time-lessness is a convenient belief, as it means that the inclusion of Shakespeare's work need not be justified, texts are relatively inexpensive and easy to acquire, and, especially recently, the popular media obligingly supply plenty of signals that studying Shakespeare is a fun and profitable thing to do. At the point of teaching, however, we think the degree to which a Shakespearean play means something stable is something that teachers should think, at least to themselves, is an open question.

In this paper, we first discuss the theory of education that underlies our belief that indeterminacy is a valuable characteristic of literature that is made the object of study.

Then we consider some of the levels on which indeterminacy exists in a Shakespearean play, taking, for example, *Romeo and Juliet*. Finally, we comment briefly on the price exacted by the double consciousness of this kind of teaching.

We write this paper as educators who have worked together directing theses for candidates for the Masters of Arts in Teaching in a liberal arts institution in the United States. We are interested in how our students have used Shakespeare to help their students play intellectually, and we have been struck by how Shakespeare's work is both a revered part of the canon and an occasion for this intellectual play.[1] In constituting for educators a place that is both canonized as conveying traditionally valuable knowledge and, at the same time, accommodating of pedagogical strategies that can introduce students to intellectual risk, Shakespeare's plays seem to us now to be particularly crucial elements of a curriculum.

I

In his recent book *In Over Our Heads – The Mental Demands of Modern Life*, Robert Kegan argues that what he calls the curriculum of modern life is so complicated that many of us are 'in over our heads' when we try to deal with the experiences of this postmodern world. He defines the obligations of adult life as parenting and partnering, work, and self-expansion and describes the mental capabilities we need to negotiate these demands (1994: 5). While his book focuses on the adult 'curriculum,' his analysis suggests that often both adults and adolescents are expected to think about and act upon ideas and mental demands that they are not prepared to meet.

Kegan's ideas can be contested, but they are provocative. He outlines ways of knowing the world which he calls levels of consciousness and posits that adults need to develop 'a fifth-order consciousness' in order to meet the multiple demands of adult life. For Kegan a fifth-order consciousness recognises the incompleteness of one's view and is in constant dialogue with opposing views and other ways to see the world. In fact, fifth-order thinking 'is suspicious of any sense of wholeness' (1994: 311).

If we take this view of adult development seriously, we recognize how difficult it is to think in a sophisticated manner. In order to do this, we might feel constantly uncertain, and that is a difficult way to live.[2] Kegan argues that adults are as unprepared for this order of thinking as adolescents are for the level of consciousness expected of them.

If Kegan is correct and adult thinking requires an awareness of the incompleteness of our views, young adults need to be helped to understand how to acknowledge uncertainty and transform the fear of it into a resolve for further thought. They can not enter adulthood believing that good thinking produces ideas that are black or white, right or wrong, complete or incomplete. Nor can they believe that all ideas are relative.[3] The hard work must begin before adulthood, learning how to think about ideas, how to construct knowledge, and how to evaluate ideas and knowledge so one can live with both the sense of incompleteness that Kegan describes and a sense that this uncertainty, if carefully evaluated, is both intellectually and personally worth the discomfort.

Curiosity, the capacity to develop one's own questions, and the ability to acknowledge that one's understanding is incomplete seem prerequisites for approaching the complexities of adult thinking. These are attributes of a mind that is active, that is not satisfied with simply receiving information. To be curious about what one learns, to develop one's own questions is to have the potential of knowing that other people may ask different questions, may be curious about something else. To be able to sit with uncertainty in a classroom is to be more likely able to sustain a sense that one's view is incomplete as an adult.

Some educational theorists suggest ways that we can teach young people, not only to know some things, but to be uncertain of other ideas and to be comfortable with that uncertainty some of the time.

In her book *Children's Minds*, Margaret Donaldson writes that if a visitor 'who knew nothing about our society' observed a preschool, she would see a Utopian community and that community would have disappeared from view if that visitor visited a high school. That preschool learning community is characterised by curiosity, and Donaldson's argument is that we educate curiosity out of our students in schools (1978: ix, x). By this she means that we teach students to forget the way they wondered about things as young children. They learn to work for the extrinsic rewards of grades and right answers and forget the exuberant curiosity involved in their early perceptions of the world. Donaldson's ideas might be paraphrased by saying that we teach children to forget to ask their own questions.

Eleanor Duckworth's work is focused on how teachers can help children develop intrinsic interest in material – to develop their own questions about material based on what about that material interests them. While Duckworth is not advocating doing away with a set curriculum, she is promoting using that curriculum in a way that invites children to think about it in many ways.[4] She writes that the virtue of knowing is over-rated: 'Of all the virtues related to intellectual functioning, the most passive is the virtue of knowing the right answer. Knowing the right answer requires no decisions, carries no risks, and makes no demands. It is automatic. It is thoughtless' (Duckworth 1996: 64). She believes that learning is about 'figuring something out' by developing a question and proceeding to try to answer it. This process can lead to dead ends, but 'mistakes' in the process can lead to new ways of figuring out an answer to one's own question.[5]

Duckworth calls not knowing and thinking about a way to learn it 'the having of wonderful ideas.' In her 1996 book of the same title, she proposes how teachers can teach their students to 'uncover' knowledge rather than only cover a curriculum.

This uncovering is Duckworth's metaphor for real learning, for developing one's own questions about material being studied. This kind of intellectual work is at the core of thinking. Many educational theorists from Jean Piaget and Lev Vygotsky to Duckworth, Donaldson, and Howard Gardner call this an aspect of constructing knowledge. In a later book *Teacher to Teacher*, Duckworth describes how a group of experienced teachers learn to construct knowledge for themselves. This book illustrates how even teachers who are bright and determined to teach their own students to work through ideas rather than to memorize material have difficulty with 'not knowing' themselves. It is hard intellectual work to figure something out and not know where that 'figuring out' is going to lead.

It is not our habit as teachers to ask a question to which we do not already know the answer; indeed, some scholars suggest that research on teaching reveals that teachers ask only the kinds of questions that produce literal thinking (Rubin 2002: 357). Carol Gilligan, in writing about her attempt to get students to ask questions that had no obvious answers, describes exactly this problem:

> I asked the students to pose a real question, a question to which they really wanted to know the answer ... in reflecting on the exercise, [students] wrote about the effort it took to clear out of their minds 'good questions' or 'important questions,' so as even to know what their real questions were. (1989: 8)[6]

Teachers may be reluctant to ask questions to which they have no answers because acknowledging uncertainty can make us vulnerable in the classroom; but perhaps also, like students, teachers may have difficulty knowing what their real questions are.

This is where Shakespeare comes in. His work offers opportunities to allow a lesson developed in a traditional mode – paraphrasing the language, summarising the plots, thinking about character motivations – to become one in which the mental capacities described above can begin to be put into play. It is an understatement that taking a class to the point of acknowledging uncertainty about the material under consideration is a less safe way of teaching, especially in a time when learning for information is perceived as the important educational goal; and we want to emphasise here that what we will discuss below is not intended to prescribe methods to be used by all teachers in all situations. If, however, as teachers, we can allow some of the indeterminate aspects of Shakespeare's work to surface in our own thinking, if we can bring to our preparation of a lesson a real question about the material – a real question that develops from curiosity, a desire to know something, or outright perplexity – then we will be in touch with the play in the text. And when it is appropriate to bring this play into our teaching, we can model for students how to ask questions and how to be secure even in a position of not knowing.

Vygotsky's (1978) formulation of the zone of proximal development is pertinent here: what we can do with assistance today, we can do alone tomorrow.

II

In the introduction to the first volume of the *Shakespeare Set Free* series of books 'by teachers, for teachers' about strategies for making the teaching of Shakespeare 'active, intellectual, energizing and a pleasure,' general editor Peggy O'Brien, then Director of Education at the Folger Shakespeare Library, refers to the 'delicate balance between a celebrated and complex writer and the slippery business of how people learn' (1993: xii–xiii).[7]

O'Brien's phrase does not actually assert that the complexity of the plays' text are crucial to their pedagogical value; but as an introduction to a series of chapters across three volumes containing thoughtful and imaginative strategies for teaching Shakespeare to students 'of all ability levels and reading levels, of every ethnic origin, in every kind of school,' her comment implies what we would here like to make explicit. Students can learn something significant when studying Shakespeare because what engages them will often elude their capacity to understand and explain; and cultivating their capacity to acknowledge that condition without being frightened by it while working toward a tentative answer is one of the most valuable things that education can do for them.

The experience of uncertainty that students have with Shakespeare's plays is more than just a function of their relative lack of sophistication. Indeterminacy is, to a significant degree, a feature of the plays themselves. Accordingly, teaching Shakespeare will involve the teacher in acknowledging, more or less explicitly as fits a given pedagogical moment, that it is difficult and may not be entirely possible to impose coherence or certainty on the thing that she and her students are working on together. In this frame of mind, a teacher may well find herself feeling that she is collaborating with students in her own attempts to come to terms with the play, especially, if paradoxically, in those moments when students seem the most unwilling to do that intellectual work.

The provocative difficulties students may have with a Shakespearean play can occur on various levels, with some of them being more obvious and accessible in the textbooks from which these plays are generally taught than others. Here we want to consider two general kinds, one focused primarily on language and the other involved with the elements of the play's action as they unfold in its plot.

Even when it is not metered, much of the language of the plays is poetry, and its concision and artfulness is compounded by the circumstance that its grammar and vocabulary are archaic. Many fine teachers have developed and published strategies for overcoming the strangeness of the language. Underlying some of the most interesting of these strategies is the premise that getting students to grasp the denotative meaning of a line or a speech is not the only way to help them feel intellectually engaged by it.[8]

So, through choral reading, reading accompanied by movement, and memorization, students can be brought to understand the prologue of *Romeo and Juliet*. That is, they can be brought to see that the poem is talking about what will happen in the play, that it is decorated with rhetorical strategies and verbal devices that make it sound formal, and that that formality may be related in some way to the issue of the play. But how much does that understanding acknowledge what is actually difficult about the poem?[9]

At some point, in her own consideration of the sonnet, perhaps with the help of students if they can be candid and articulate about their difficulties, the teacher might try to see the poem as they see it—not by making their difficulties her difficulties; rather, by allowing herself to experience the same *kinds* of difficulties that students have:

> Two households, both alike in dignity,
> In fair Verona, where we lay our scene,
> From ancient grudge break to new mutiny,
> Where civil blood makes civil hands unclean. (Pro. 1–4)[10]

The second of these lines intrudes grammatically on the syntax of the sentence. Is the effect one of afterthought or emphasis? And is this odd intrusion of Verona related to the curious repetition of 'civil'? Why is a fight between two households called a 'mutiny'? Does 'grudge' mean that the origin of the quarrel was a trivial incident? Who are 'we,' and why are 'we' so prominent in the poem?

> From forth the fatal loins of these two foes
> A pair of star-crossed lovers take their life;
> Whose misadventured piteous overthrows
> Doth with their death bury their parents' strife. (Pro. 5–8)

Is the poem confusing the act by which the two children are conceived (by their fathers) with the moments in which their mothers give birth to them? What relationship does this confusion have to the ambiguity whereby 'take their life,' meaning come into being, seems like a reference to suicide? Do the lovers have one life or two? (Has Shakespeare sacrificed coherence to rhyme?) Are the 'overthrows' of which the poem speaks something the lovers do or something that is done to them?

> The fearful passage of their death-marked love,
> And the continuance of their parents' rage,

Which, but their children's end, naught could remove,
Is now the two hours' traffic of our stage;
The which if you with patient ears attend,
What here shall miss, our toil shall strive to mend. (Pro. 9–14)

The first two of these lines purport to say what the play will be about, but is the implication that it is about love and continuing parental rage in equal measure? Why does the poem make its crucial assertion – that the 'children's end' is the one thing (otherwise 'naught' could do it) that can end the rage – in that parenthetical way? Why does the poem emphasise so much what we will hear, and where is the 'here' of the last line? Why would a poem that insists so much on listening use words (like 'here') that can be so easily mistaken for other words ('hear')?

We pose these questions, not to imply that the poem has richness and depth in its violently compressed language (though that is a reasonable critical judgment to make), but rather because we think they express reasons why any careful reader might be as perplexed by this prologue, though perhaps in different ways, as a student who had never seen it before and for whom many of the words and tricks of language were unfamiliar. Perhaps that perplexity is relevant to the experience of the play, but our point here is that a naïve student and a very sophisticated reader who encountered this poem without already knowing what it says and how it relates to the play it supposedly introduces might have similar reactions to it, though one would be considerably more confident of her reaction than the other.

The process, then, of bringing students to the point where they feel they understand the poem well enough to paraphrase it may impose a coherence on it that it does not have. It may not be always appropriate to share that perception with students; but a teacher who acknowledges it will respect her students' difficulties with it and become, through confronting those difficulties, more attentive to the astonishing stylistic features of the poem and the play it introduces. Perhaps more importantly the teacher will articulate real questions about the play. In fact, a careful reading of this sonnet is as likely to multiply the questions it raises, as it is to resolve its elements into a single coherent interpretation.

The often opaque quality of Shakespeare's language is equalled by a corresponding density of what we might call a play's plot. In any account of the story that a play presents, scenes or parts of scenes or even entire characters assume a different emphasis than they have in the text of the play. Some examples of what appear to be overdone or extraneous elements of *Romeo and Juliet* include the full extent of the nurse's lamentations and the musicians quarrelling with Peter after Juliet is discovered presumably dead in Act IV. Teachers can use productions to locate such moments. Filmed productions, in particular, streamline the action; and what is consistently omitted from them can be the occasion of asking students if their sense of the play takes into account such apparently eccentric or unnecessary moments. What is the result of representing the reaction to Juliet's false death to the point of bathos if not comedy? Did Shakespeare make a mistake here, go too far in establishing that grief for Juliet's death was premature? Or is the experience we call tragedy more incoherent than it seems in the abstract?

Furthermore, to an extent that is belied by the editions out of which we now teach them, many of Shakespeare's plays present anomalies in the action that have been simply dismissed in order to rationalize the stories that the plays represent.[11] One of them will serve here to describe the kind of issues that emerge from an awareness of how our sense of 'what Shakespeare wrote' is fashioned out of the evidence of early printed editions that can seem confusing and in conflict with one another.

At issue in this anomaly is the critical moment in the play when the Prince arrives to find Tybalt dead, Romeo fled, and those remaining on the scene telling him that the death of Tybalt occurred at Romeo's hand, not because Romeo, as a Montague, essentially hates Capulets, but because Tybalt had, in a scuffle that Romeo himself tried to prevent, killed Mercutio, the Prince's kinsman. Lady Capulet disputes the account of Benvolio:

> He is a kinsman to the Montague;
> Affection makes him false, he speaks not true.
> Some twenty of them fought in this black strife,
> And all those twenty could but take one life.
> I beg for justice, which thou, Prince, must give.
> Romeo slew Tybalt; Romeo must not live. (III.i.178–83)

This interpretation of events gives the Prince pause:

> Romeo slew him; he slew Mercutio.
> Who now the price of his dear blood doth owe? (III.i.184–85)

The question posed by the Prince seems affected by the same uncertainty that perplexes us in the prologue-sonnet. 'His dear blood doth owe': whose blood is owed for this crime? Or who is he whose blood must be requited? Someone speaks to resolve the by-no-means clearly stated conundrum:

> Not Romeo, Prince; he was Mercutio's friend;
> His fault concludes but what the law should end,
> The life of Tybalt. (III.i.186–88)

Seeming to defend Romeo, the speaker of this speech might reasonably be assumed to be Romeo's father, to whom the speech is assigned in most editions of the play, following a version of the play printed probably in 1622, nearly three decades after the play was written and first performed.

The problem arises because the first several times the speech was printed, when Shakespeare was alive and working in the theatre, the speech is assigned to Capulet, Tybalt's uncle and Juliet's father. Moreover, when the play was printed in the First Folio of Shakespeare's plays, published in 1623, seven years after his death, by two members of the company with which he worked, it is the assignment to Capulet, not Montague, that the text records. For the next one hundred years, most readers of the play read Capulet, not Montague, as the person who argues that Romeo did only what justice itself would have done, take Tybalt's life for killing Mercutio.

What did Shakespeare write? We cannot know. Did he change his mind? We likewise can only surmise. What difference does it make? It makes a very considerable difference if we read this play as a representation of the actions of people locked in the implacable hatred of one clan for another. Seeing the speech as assigned alternatively to Montague and Capulet raises questions about human behaviour in such circumstances.

These are questions to be asked of our students. The education we need depends on teachers finding ways to convey to their students that answers can be only provisional, embraced 'wholeheartedly' (Perry 1981), passionately justified in a close reading of the text, and understood as liable to be qualified by the uncertainties that, by design or happenstance, characterise Shakespeare's plays.

III

Teaching Shakespeare the way we have here discussed involves developing divergent ways to think in both teachers and students. It is a matter of both 'doing Shakespeare,' in the idiom of U.S. English, and undoing him: giving our students the wherewithal to make sense of his plays and acknowledging, at the same time, that the structure and language of the plays themselves do not wholly accommodate the coherence we need to impose on them.

The undoing part is the harder, of course, for by teaching in this way we must undo the ways both we and our students have learned to think and to measure academic success. For teachers, it must also be said, the work of undoing takes time and resources. Taking the risk of acknowledging the countermotions in the language and plot of a well-known Shakespeare play is an activity that, in an ideal world, would be supported by opportunities for further education and teacher development. In the United States, in the world of public education, these resources are in short supply.

Yet if we take seriously the need to prepare our children for the complex thinking that will be required of them as adults, we should contrive a way, in the midst of even the most unimaginative discourse about public education, to create classrooms in which teachers can help students develop the courage to take intellectual risks, to ask their own questions, to play intellectually as preparation for the important work of being parents and citizens of their local communities and of the world. In this, Shakespeare, good, old, safe, canonical, and ultimately mysterious Shakespeare, is a most useful ally.

Sara Lawrence Lightfoot says good teachers live in a world of ideas. Ideas are not 'right answers.' They are the imaginative leaps we make when certainty is nowhere in sight.

Notes

1   A version of this paper was presented at a meeting of the National Council of Teachers of English in Chicago, March 1998. At the NCTE Shakespeare Y2K Conference in March 2000 in Bethesda, Maryland, Susan Schoonmaker's Master-of-Arts-in-Teaching thesis, *Theatre as Moral Education*, was the subject of a panel in which we, as its directors, participated. We would like to acknowledge the valuable responses of Schoonmaker and all the teachers who participated in these sessions.

2   The idea that it is difficult but necessary to live with uncertainty is acknowledged in popular culture as well as academic philosophy. A philosophical articulation of the importance and difficulty of this condition is an argument of Martha Nussbaum's *Cultivating Humanity*.

3   See William Perry for one discussion about the dangers of relativistic thinking.

4   'Invites' is a word that Nel Noddings uses in speaking about curriculum.

5   Howard Gardner (1985) suggests that intelligence is problem posing as much as it is problem solving. He and Duckworth thus agree on the importance of curiosity, the quality emphasized by Donaldson. While Duckworth writes about teaching and learning and Gardner's book questions what intelligence is, they have in common the belief that not knowing something is a 'virtue,' in Duckworth's words.

6   Gilligan (1989) discusses this point in a description of her class on clinical interviewing, and she is speaking specifically about the experience of women in this course.

7   *Shakespeare Set Free: Teaching* Romeo and Juliet, Macbeth, *and* A Midsummer Night's Dream, ed. Peggy O'Brien, is the first of a series of three collections that emerged from the Teaching Shakespeare Institute of the Folger Shakespeare Library. See also *Shakespeare Set Free: Teaching* Hamlet *and* Henry IV Part I *and* Shakespeare Set Free: Teaching *Twelfth Night and* Othello. Lesson plans that have emerged out of more recent Teaching Shakespeare Institutes at the Folger are available at http://www.folger.edu/education/teaching.htm.

8   A forthcoming article by Janet Field-Pickering (2002), current Head of Education at the Folger, describes some techniques for making the language accessible. See also, *passim*, the lesson plans of the Teaching Shakespeare Institute mentioned in note 7 above and Rex Gibson and Janet Field-Pickering (1998).

9   The approach to the language of the plays taken here owes much to the work of Stephen Booth. That said, it should, however, be acknowledged that Booth would likely be more persuaded than we now are that *Romeo and Juliet* is, in all of its parts, manifestly coherent. For teachers involved in a curriculum that must embrace lots of things besides Shakespeare, perhaps the best introduction to Booth's stimulating and provocative habits of reading are in his book *Precious Nonsense: The Gettysburg Address, Ben Jonson's Epitaphs on his Children, and Twelfth Night.*

10 Lines from Romeo and Juliet quoted in this essay are taken from the text of the play in the Signet Classic edition of the play. Incidentally, this edition is one of the few modern editions that assigns the lines discussed below to Capulet.

11 Jill Levenson (2000) discusses some of the many issues that emerge about the play once the various readings that are contained in early printed forms are taken into account. She does not discuss this point, however, because her essay is about the first quarto of the play, where the speech in question does not occur.

References

Booth, S. (1998) *Precious Nonsense: The Gettysburg Address, Ben Jonson's Epitaphs on his Children, and Twelfth Night*, Berkeley: Univ. of California Press.

Donaldson, M. (1978) *Children's Minds*, New York: W.W. Norton.

Duckworth, E. (1996) *The Having of Wonderful Ideas*, New York: Teachers College Press.

Duckworth, E. (1997) *Teacher to Teacher*, New York: Teachers College Press.

Field-Pickering, J. (2002) 'Shakespeare Steps Out: The Primacy of Language in Inner-City Classrooms', Miller, N. (ed) *A Local Habitation and a Name: Re-imagining Shakespeare for Children and Young Adults*, forthcoming from Routledge.

Gardner, H. (1983) *Frames of Mind*, New York: Basic Books.

Gibson, R. and J. Field-Pickering (1998) *Discovering Shakespeare's Language: 150 Stimulating Activity Sheets for Student Work*, New York: Cambridge University Press.

Gilligan, C. (1989) 'Teaching Shakespeare's Sister', Gilligan, C., Lyons, N., and Hanmer, T. (eds) *Making Connections: The Relational Worlds of Adolescent Girls at Emma Willard School*, Troy, New York: Emma Willard, 6–19.

Kegan, R. (1994) *In Over Our Heads*, Cambridge: Harvard University Press.

Levenson, J. (2000) 'Teaching the Books of the Play', Hunt, M. (ed) *Approaches to Teaching Shakespeare's* Romeo and Juliet, New York: Modern Language Association, 153–62.

Lightfoot, S. L. (1988) 'An Interview with Bill Moyers' *A World of Ideas*, PBS TV, Adult Learning Series, Alexandria, Virginia.

Noddings, N. (1999) 'Schools and Social Justice,' Public lecture, Colgate University.

Nussbaum, M. (1994) *Cultivating Humanity*, Cambridge: Harvard University Press.

Perry, W. G. (1981) 'Cognitive and Ethical Growth: The Making of Meaning', Chickering, A. (ed) *Modern American College*, San Francisco: Jossey-Bass, 76–116.

Piaget, J. (1937/1986) *The Construction of Reality in the Child* (M. Cook, trans.), New York: Ballantine.

Rubin, D. (2002) *Diagnosis and Correction in Reading Instruction*, Boston: Allyn and Bacon.

Schoonmaker, S. (1999) *Theatre as Moral Education* Master of Arts in Teaching Thesis, Hamilton, New York: Colgate University.

Shakespeare Set Free: Teaching Romeo and Juliet, Macbeth, *and* A Midsummer Night's Dream (1993) O'Brien, P. (ed) New York: Washington Square Press.

Shakespeare Set Free: Teaching Hamlet *and* Henry IV, Part I (1994) O'Brien, P. (ed) New York: Washington Square Press.

Shakespeare Set Free: Teaching Twelfth Night *and* Othello (1995) O'Brien, P. (ed) New York: Washington Square Press.

Shakespeare, W. (1998) *The Tragedy of Romeo and Juliet*, Bryant, J. A. (ed) New York: Penguin.

'Teaching Shakespeare' (2001) http://www.folger.edu/education/teaching.htm (accessed 19 April 2002).

Vgotsky, L. (1978) *Mind in Society*, Cambridge: Harvard University Press.

11

Studying the
Art of Provoking

Pavel Drábek

Whatever you purport to say about a thing, you're only expressing your own beliefs. (M. Minsky, *The Society of Mind*, in Varela 1991: 142)

While observing the interaction of other people, be it in real life or on the stage, we automatically recall our own motoric experiences without being conscious of it, and we recall them the more extensively and powerfully the more we *identify* ourselves with their interactions in our imagination, which we obviously do when perceiving a stage performance. (Zich 1931: 48)[1]

Without me as within me; not imagined, felt. (*Cymbeline* IV.ii.309)[2]

This chapter presents a set of approaches used for the analysis and interpretation of Shakespearean drama. The entire method is based on what Zich (1931) calls the 'noetic' of theatre, that is, focusing on the cognitive aspect of experiencing a play while reading it. In other words, it is a study of the ways in which the reader as a potential spectator accepts, acquires, builds up, understands, and experiences the play. From the noetic point of view, plays do not exist on the paper, nor in fact on the stage. They arise in the spectator's or reader's mind as a sequence of associations suggested or provoked by impeti from the stage or the page. The theoretical background of this approach is based on the latest methods of cognitive science – the 'embodied experience' (Varela et al. 1991) – on the one hand, and the Zich 'school' of dramatic and theatrical semiotics (Zich 1931; Osolsobě 1974) on the other. What all of these approaches share is their focus on the experiencing subject, the individual with his/her own capacity for experiencing.

Some of these approaches may be used on individual plays, others comparatively. The case studies that follow involve the portrayal of the 'Shrew' in two plays – Shakespeare's *The Taming of the Shrew* (?1589–94), and the anonymous *The Taming of a Shrew* (printed in 1594) – and two comparable Jacobean plays, Shakespeare's *The Tempest* (1611), and Fletcher and Massinger's *The Sea Voyage* (c1622).

I

The most efficient way of summing up the effect of a tragedy is to consider which elements of the story Shakespeare has shown on stage and how he has done so. (Brown 1996: 155)

Once we realise that a play needs to be self-contained, that is, it is in a sense the foundation and only source of its story, involving plot, characters, and so forth, we can then understand that it has certain given, obligatory technical, constructive functions. At the same time, theatre is entertainment, and the play (meaning both the dramatist's and the producer's/director's work) needs to obey certain publicly acceptable limits of communicating. For example: realistic theatre ruled out chorus-figures and behaving out of character; different societies react differently to moralistic, sermon-like speeches; and nowadays, exaggerated pathos, or sentimentalism, popular up until the earlier twentieth century, is unacceptable.

Studying a play from the point of how it is constructed helps understand the dramatist's art and abilities. For the purpose of getting closer to the structure, it is useful to make two kinds of abstracts of a play: one is the *argument*, that is, a summary of the story in prose; the other is the scenario, an outline of scenes and their happenings. This 'back-forming' is by all means a legitimate procedure; there is a strong argument that the *plat* (or *plotte*) – as it was called in early modern England – was a more or less standard halfway stage in the process of composition of a play.

This *plat*, in its map-like generalisation, makes possible a whole range of critical approaches. Some of them relate to the *plat* itself: How is the story (summed up in the *argument*) portioned up into the *plat*? Where does the plot of the play begin? How does the 'plotter' build up the story? How does he/she move the action forward? What is shown on the stage, in terms of what is presented and what is in turn omitted? What are the possible merits of such choices? Or, in the words of Ellis-Fermor,

Why does Shakespeare not give us the murder of Duncan? ... There are wide gaps in the sequence ... This becomes clear when we consider what is in fact omitted in some of the greatest of his plays from the material he might have used, material that a lesser dramatist would have considered suitable or even highly effective in its theatrical and rhetorical effects. (1960: 79, 77)

How is the balancing of scenes worked out? What is the proportion and ordering of 'light entertainment' and 'grave matter'? How are music and spectacle distributed throughout the play? How do these support, or go against, the action and the sentiment of the play?

In the course of such an analysis, students may make many varied and plausible suggestions in response to these questions. Naturally, all such responses are speculation and ought to be taken as such, yet speculation has some power of illumination in all its unfoundedness. Although we may never be sure of the author's purpose, in the conjectures a certain 'space' for possible intentions opens up. The play itself is thus the manifestation of the unattainable, though inherent purpose.

Drama, or some kinds of drama, tends to conceal its necessary technical functions, such as providing the exposition and projection – that is, anticipating what might happen or is about to happen – communicating information essential for the understanding, as well as a fair amount of redundancy (Hall 1998). At the beginning of a drama, be it a whole play or a scene only, the audience needs to become oriented in the dramatic (fictive) happenings. This may be achieved by technical characters such as T. S. Eliot's

… attendant lord, one that will do
To swell a progress, start a scene or two (1963: 17, lines 112–13)

Or, these technical functions may be concealed and fulfilled as if by the way. Students can then be asked: what is the measure of 'technicality' in the analysed play? Shakespeare, in some of his plays, achieves an outstanding level of 'non-technicality', or one might say, 'realism', particularly in his middle plays, where he manages to weave the technical elements into the – rather natural – dialogue and characterisation. His last plays – and their 'continuation' into the Fletcherian canon[3] – however, do not follow this direction; from the point of realism, they are a certain step backwards. Why so? What are their 'new' objectives?

A step closer from the structure of the *plat* to the actual playtext is an analysis of the ways the author communicates off-stage happenings. Does he use a chorus figure? If such happenings are mediated by the characters, what is their motivation for doing so? How does the information they are delivering influence their character? Does the dramatist or character withhold something from the audience or the other characters, and if so, why? A considerably complex question involves the proportion of visuality to aurality: how much of the play is physical action and how much of it is speech?

Another relevant object of study is the *compositional* aspect: how does the dramatist realise the *plat*? Given the purpose of the scene (clearly to be found in the *plat*), how is this purpose brought out? What is the structure of the scene? How is it developed?[4] However, a scene must be constructed as a full-fledged utterance (in the linguistic sense); in other words, there is no 'difference between a *scene* and a *play* … The basic elements involved in a scene or in a play are the same' (Hall 1998: 112). So how does an analysis focusing on the realisation of the scene's purpose go together with the 'technical' construction of the scene?[5]

All action happens at a concrete time and in a concrete place. However, on the stage there is a certain amount of 'timelessness' and 'nowhere-ness'. Very often we even do not need to know where or when something happens; we are simply interested in what happens. With time, it is enough for us to assume that the next 'event' happens 'later on', unless the dramatist needs to specify it. If he/she does so, why is it? Sometimes this may be for verisimilitude's sake, or to emphasise the *here and now* of the onstage action; sometimes it serves the coherence of our understanding (it may help the exposition), sometimes both; for example:

> [*Hamlet to Horatio et al.*]   So fare ye well.
> Upon the platform 'twixt eleven and twelve
> I'll visit you. (*Hamlet* I.ii.250–52)

or again:

> *Enter* PRINCE HAMLET, HORATIO, *and* MARCELLUS
> *Hamlet.* The air bites shrewdly, it is very cold.
> *Horatio.* It is a nipping and an eager air.
> *Hamlet.* What hour now?
> *Horatio.* I think it lacks of twelve.
> *Marcellus.* No, it is struck.
> *Horatio.* Indeed? I heard it not. (I.iv.1–6)

One thing about dramatic time should be borne in mind. Early modern drama is strictly chronological; things coming after happen later. Fiction runs in several lines (plots). At a performance, the onstage action is a linear sequence of events only. The dramatist may even 'violate' the fiction a bit in what is known as the double time scheme. While reading the play, this discrepancy may be oppressive; in theatre, however, much of our attention is given to the onstage happenings, and lapses in time are often either unnoticed, or understood as of no importance.

Similarly, we often find ourselves with no place specified. This happens regularly in reflective monologues or informative exchanges, such as between the Earl of Kent and the First Gentleman in the Q text of *King Lear*, Scene 17; at other times, we infer a place. And sometimes we are intentionally left *in no place*. That is where the first dialogue between Hamlet and the Ghost takes place. Moreover, we are expressly made aware of the place-lessness by Horatio:

> *Horatio.* What if it tempt you toward the flood, my lord,
> Or to the dreadful summit of the cliff
> That beetles o'er his base into the sea,
> And there assume some other horrible form
> Which might deprive your sovereignty of reason
> And draw you into madness? Think of it. (I.iv.50–55)

Where do dialogues with ghosts take place? Is it coincidence that Horatio warns Marcellus and us that 'He [Hamlet] waxes desperate with imagination' (1.4.64)? In the following scene, place is stressed again; however, without identification:

> *Enter the* GHOST*, and* PRINCE HAMLET *following*
> *Hamlet.* Whither wilt thou lead me? Speak. I'll go no further. (I.v.1)

Similarly, an analysis focused on the study of time and space as they are suggested in the playtext (and therefore presumably on the stage) can reveal not only the dimensions of the play but also, of course, opportunities for judging the dramatist's achievement. Similarly, students may analyse how characters are built, taking into consideration self-characterisation (conscious and unconscious) and instances of indirect characterisation by other people in the play. Depending on the students' and the teacher's practical theatrical experience, suggestions (and ideally attempts at realisation) can be made as to how a certain passage could be acted or presented on the stage. Questions such as which decisions are more aesthetically appealing, and why, might then be addressed.

II

All the above approaches can be applied comparatively as well. Let us take a brief look at two versions of the Shrew: Shakespeare's Katherine in *The Taming of the Shrew*, and Kate in the anonymous *The Taming of a Shrew* (c.1594), and see what we can learn about them. (Here the focus will be on the anonymous play, with Shakespeare's play taken into consideration implicitly.)

In *The Taming of a Shrew*,[6] Aurelius, on coming to Athens and meeting his friend Polidor, sees Alphonsus' three daughters – 'dames ... so bright of hew/Whose eies are brighter then the lampes of heauen' (*A Shrew* 170–71) – on their way to church, while their father is after 'Marchandise' (177). Aurelius takes 'much delight' (181) in them, and learns from Polidor that the father

> [...] hath solemnlie sworne,
>
> His eldest daughter first shall be espowsde
>
> [...] And he that hath her shall be fettred so,
>
> As good be wedded to the diuell himselfe,
>
> For such a skould as she did neuer lieu (*A Shrew* 193–200)

Polidor instantly proceeds to the point:

> We must deuise a meanes and find some one
>
> That will attempt to wed this deuilish skould,
>
> And I doo know the man. (215–17)

If the shrew is to be a real shrew, she has to be dramatised properly. Polidor knew of Ferando (the tamer) before the play started. And yet he makes much fuss about finding the daring man, and waits till the audience gets the whole chunk of the expositional material. If the man is found with so little effort, the problem is not so difficult and unsolvable, and therefore the 'skould' is not so haggish as they claim. By such a quick solution, the audience is deprived of the pleasure of relishing Kate's asocialness, the pleasure of suspense, and – broadly – the pleasure of enjoying the situation, not to mention the lack of interaction, or – indeed – communication, between Polidor and Aurelius in the expositional scene; and Aurelius's falling in love in the midst of his verbosity.

The dramatist avoids a direct portrayal of what Kate really is: she is not shown in her family during the exposition; even a scene in which Polidor and Aurelius would be persuading Ferando to court her is lacking. When Ferando enters for the first time, he is on his way 'To bonie *Kate*, the patientst wench aliue' (252), adding the expositional 'The diuel himselfe dares scarce venter to woo her' (253), concluding 'And she and I must woo with skoulding sure' (257). We are robbed of dramatic conflict; Polidor almost seems to apologise for the absence of the scene of persuading:

> *Polidor.* How like you this *Aurelius*, I thinke he knew
>
> Our mindes before we sent to him[.] (260–61)

Kate is dramatised as already rather tame; there is nothing really shrewish about her. Only somewhat later does her shrewishness come across. Even so, it relies mostly on her quick repartee:

> *Kate.* Let go my hand, for feare it reach your eare.
> [...]
> *Alfonso.* How now Ferando, what saies my daughter?
> *Ferando.* Shees willing sir and loues me as hir life.
> *Kate.* Tis for your skin then, but not to be your wife. (304–10)

For all her nimble tongue, there is something harmless about her and her behaviour. One realises this when she addresses her father plaintively, and at the same time, wills something different:

> *Kate.* Why father, what do you meane to do with me,
> To giue me thus vnto this brainsick man,
> That in his mood cares not to murder me?
> *She turnes aside and speakes.*
> But yet I will consent and marrie him,
> For I methinkes haue liude too long a maid,
> And match him to, or else his manhoods good. (314–19)

(How, we wonder, did she get the idea of murder?) Despite all the ado, she is quite pliable and ready to consent, giving us a considerably implausible (because unprepared) reason for her decision. In the parallel situation in Shakespeare's play, Katherine is shrewish, yet flattered by Petruccio's advances; the way her assent is prepared is not so clear-cut and rational, which leaves space for a reason behind her behaviour, a reason that we may guess at but never know for certain. It is in the comparison to the anonymous Kate that we may realise what character Shakespeare creates: Katherine waiting for her bridegroom says, 'Would Katherine had never seen him, though', and '*Exit weeping*' (III.ii.26). This may be acted as embarrassment and shame, but there is arguably more to it: Katherine seems to have an emotional tie to Petruccio by now.

In the anonymous *Shrew*, there are a number of puzzling moments in the form of dramatic lapses, such as the reason why Ferando has to 'hie to my countrie house' (327) when he has a house in Athens (from which he enters for the scene at 217). Later in the play, there is no obvious reason for the teacher of music to be introduced; Polidor claims it is to make Kate busy so that her sisters have 'time to steale abrode' (428). But why so much fuss about a day that is to elapse before the wedding? The music lesson is necessarily a failure, and yet the teacher refers to a previous one: 'play the lesson that I taught you last' (478). It seems that it is there for the trick with the lute, the little shrewish action that Kate is allowed: '*She offers to strike him with the lute*' (501) and '*She throwes it downe*' (504).[7]

In this case, a comparative approach reveals that in general, the anonymous *Shrew* betrays signs of inferiority in that it disrupts the unity of the story for the sake of attractive spectacle.[8] The play is not constructed to create 'plasticity' of character and dramatic situation as in Shakespeare's play, but rather as a vehicle for conspicuous stage sensation.

III

The so-called Fletcherian canon contains a number of 'derivative' plays that often re-use Shakespearean material.[9] Some critics have considered them epigonic works,[10] or – in the better case – parodies. However, there are sufficient grounds to consider them rather as artistic *ripostes*, offering a different perspective or a differing view of Shakespeare's subject matter. One such *riposte* is John Fletcher and Philip Massinger's *The Sea Voyage* (1622), a reaction to Shakespeare's *The Tempest*. In the following paragraphs, I would like to concentrate on the significance of the storm and the island within the two plays; comparing and contrasting Shakespeare's storm and island with the Fletcherian ones helps to establish the fundamental difference between the two plays, as in both the significance of weather and topography plays a crucial role. Following the ways in which the plays' characters interpret the storm and the island may help uncover the characteristics of each play and suggest possible ways of evaluating each one.

In *The Sea Voyage*, the storm scenes on board the ship are more naturalistic, and more satirical at the same time. For the lovers – the captain Albert and the kidnapped Aminta – the storm is a punishment of heaven on the kidnapper, as Aminta makes explicit:

> [*Aminta.*] O Mounsier Albert, How am I bound to curse ye,
> If curses could redeeme me? how to hate ye?
> You forc't me from my quiet, from my friends;
> [...] You forc't my friends from their peacefull rest,
> Some your relentles sword gave their last groanes;
> [...] Was this a lovers part? but heaven has found ye,
> And in his lowd voyce, his voyce of thunder,
> And in the mutiny of his deep wonders,
> He tels ye now, ye weepe too late (*SV* 1.94–111)

The satirist Tibalt, and the merchant La-mure give the storm another significance:

> *Master.* It must all over boord. [...]
> *La-mure.* Must my goods over too?
> Why honest Master? here lies all my money;

The money I ha wrackt by usurie,
To buy new Lands and Lordships in new Countryes,
'Cause I was banisht from mine own
I ha been this tweenty yeers a raising it.
Tibalt.   Out with it:
The devils are got together by the eares, who shall have it;
And here they quarrell in the clouds.
La-mure.   I am undone Sir:
Tibalt. And be undone, 'tis better then we perish.
La-mure. O save one Chest of Plate.
Tibalt.   A way with it, lustily Saylors;
It was some pawne, that he has got unjustly;
Down with it low enough, and let Crabs breed in't (*SV* 1.128–49)

For La-mure, this storm results in the loss of the object of his covetousness; it is a punishment for the impure means by which he got his wealth, as Tibalt explicates. In this
scene La-mure is a variant of the medieval Mercator, the Latin version of Everyman,
who loses his worldly goods when face-to-face with death. In a sense, Tibalt – as the
fool – plays the role of Death:

La-mure.   Sir you may loose too.
Tibalt. Thou liest; I ha nothing but my skinne,
And my Clothes; my sword here, and my self;
Two Crowns in my Pocket; two paire of Cards;
And three false Dice: I can swime like a Fish;
Rascall, nothing to hinder me. (*SV* 1.161–66)

And that is the end of their exchange: no retort, no objection allowed.

In the second scene, the castaways Sebastian and his nephew Nicusa introduce
themselves as those at the very bottom, castaways who have lost all, and whom no
tribulation can affect:

Nicusa. To still and quiet minds, that knew no misery,
It may seeme wretched, but with us 'tis ordinary;
Heaven has no Storm in store, nor earth no terror,
That can seeme new to us. (*SV* 1.176–79)

They watch the ship 'make to harbour', and foresee the affliction of the seamen to
follow:

Nicusa. Most miserable men; I greive their Fortunes.

Sebastian. How happy had they been, had the Sea cover'd 'em?

They leap from one calamity to another;

Had they been drown'd, they had ended all their sorrows.

What showts of joy they make?

Nicusa. Alas poor wretches, had they but once experience

Of this Island, they'd turn their tunes to waylings;

Sebastian. Nay, to curses. (*SV* 1.189–96)

This island is a purgatory, where for anybody there is 'nothing to restore him,/But heavenly hopes' (1.202–03). When the seamen arrive, Sebastian explains to them (1.442–52) that they became castaways after a lethal fight for the 'cursed Gold', which is on the island in abundance, and urges the newcomers 'O be you wise and carefull' (1.452). In the skirmish for gold that follows his words, Sebastian and Nicusa steal the ship and escape with it. They flee the purgatory once they lost their covetousness of gold:

Nicusa. Away deer Uncle.

Sebastian. This Gold was our overthrow.

Nicusa. It may now be our happinesse.   *Ex.* (*SV* 1.463–65)

Shakespeare's island in *The Tempest* is of a different kind, though similar in some ways. It is to the newcomers that the island seems an unbearable affliction:

Gonzalo. All torment, trouble, wonder, and amazement

Inhabits here. Some heavenly power guide us

Out of this fearful country! (*Tempest* V.i.106–08)

The old inhabitants see the place differently:

[*Miranda.*] What foul play had we that we came from thence?

Or blessèd was't we did?

Sebastian.   Both, both, my girl.

By foul play, as thou sayst, were we heaved thence,

But blessedly holp hither. (I.ii.60–63)

Unlike *The Sea Voyage*, in which the motive for Sebastian and Nicusa's (unambiguous) affliction is very concrete, in *The Tempest* it is left unpronounced, thus giving scope to figurative, metaphoric or symbolic, meanings:

[*Prospero.*] I, thus neglecting worldly ends, [...]
in my false brother
Awaked an evil nature; and my trust,
Like a good parent, did beget of him
A falsehood (I.ii.89–95)

It is rather important that Prospero lays blame on himself, namely to his 'neglecting [of] worldly ends'. This neglect awakes an evil nature and a falsehood. No other specification. Later it develops into 'ambition' (I.ii.105) and a greed for power. The evil brother, Antonio, 'only' seizes the opportunity, assisted by Alonso. A parallel to this archetypal situation occurs in the very next scene (II.i), when Ariel, led by Prospero, offers such an opportunity to Sebastian, assisted by the tempter Antonio.

In *The Sea Voyage*, it is the island itself (and its desertedness) that afflicts those who are on it, not the man-imposed charm of *The Tempest*. Here, as in Fletcher and Massinger's *The Prophetess* (1622), there is an obvious shift from a supernatural providence to the secular analogy, self-affliction through vice.[11] The supernatural providence is represented by Prospero's magic, which secures justice in the form of a punishment for unnaturalness. In *The Sea Voyage*, the covetous punish themselves – as the authors make clear to the audience. Prospero's island is metaphorical in what it sets right. The other island is – at least in the first part of *The Sea Voyage* – a concrete punishment on the greedy, who make themselves captive on it through their adherence to money.

IV

there is nothing either good or bad but thinking makes it so. (Hamlet II.ii.251–52)

In effect, these 'noetic' approaches do not differ radically from other types of intrinsic critical approaches; however, focusing on the objective knowledge as traceable in the text helps separate what is actually in the play from the associations it stimulates in our minds. The study of the processes of cognition helps 'constructively decompose' the idea of the unapproachable myth (the dramatist's art), and find the boundaries between the objective effect and the subjective response. In other words, these methods analyse what techniques and tricks the dramatist uses to provoke the play in our mind. Consequently, one may ask: How does the art of provoking differ from author to author? Is there a sense of superior and inferior techniques? What are the criteria for dramatic achievement?

One setback of the method is its considerable, almost 'inhuman', technicality if pursued too rigorously. The fact that the noetic approach focuses on the *objective* information might prevent the student from investing the text with the human, emotional responses of excitement and pleasure. In practice, however, this is no substantial problem; the technical approach may take as its point of departure the pre-critical, emotional response, and analyse what it was that objectively contributed to our impression. In the end, and ideally, it is the Horacian 'useful [did he mean 'relevant'?] pleasure' that we wish to get from drama.

Notes

1 I am quoting from an unpublished translation of Zich's *Aesthetic of the Dramatic Art*, made by Samuel Kostomlatský, revised by Ivo Osolsobě, and *ad hoc* by me. I would like to thank Prof. Osolsobě for kindly lending me his private copy of the translation. The page numbering refers, however, to the first Czech edition of 1931.

2 All references to Shakespeare's plays are from Wells and Taylor (1988), *The Oxford Shakespeare*.

3 See note 7

4 See also Emrys Jones's (1971) work on the scenic form in Shakespeare.

5 For this issue, see also Ellis-Fermor 1960.

6 Hereafter cited as *A Shrew*, followed by the appropriate line number(s). The original edition of the play has 'through-line numbering' (TLN), i.e. continuous lineation throughout.

7 The lack of plausible motivation for arbitrary happenings, such as the music lesson motive or Aurelio's disguise, supports the hypothesis that it is *A Shrew* that came second, only after Shakespeare's play. It may be noted that in Greene's *Orlando Furioso*, performed in c1591, the hero in his madness 'strikes and beates [a fiddler] with the fiddle', and then 'breakes it about his head' (TLN lines 1116 and 1122).

8 In Osolsobě's semiotic terminology, the play makes dominant the *theatrical* and the *dramatic function* (Osolsobě 1992: 158–64).

9 John Fletcher (1579–1625) was a prolific and, in his own time and immediately following, a renowned playwright. He is particularly noted for his collaborative work with other playwrights, especially Francis Beaumont. He also collaborated with Shakespeare on *The Two Noble Kinsmen* and *Henry VIII* (Drabble 1985: 355).

10 Epigonic: 'belonging to a later and less noteworthy generation' (*The Concise English Dictionary* 1968 Cassell, London).

11 Fletcher and Massinger's *The Prophetess* (1622) is another riposte to *The Tempest*. See my article 'The Prophetess and *Life is a Dream*: Two Early Modern Plays on Worldly Prerogative' *Brno Studies in English* 27 (2002).

References

Aristotle (1927) *Poetics*, trans. W. Hamilton Fyfe, The Loeb Classics Library, Cambridge, Mass., London: Heinemann, Harvard UP.

Brown, John Russell (1996) *William Shakespeare: Writing for Performance*, Basingstoke: Macmillan.

Drabble, Margaret, ed. (1985) *The Oxford Companion to English Literature*, 5th edn, Oxford University Press, Oxford.

Eliot, T. S. (1963) 'The Love Song of J. Alfred Prufrock' (1917), *Collected Poems 1909–1962*, London: Faber and Faber.

Ellis-Fermor, Una (1960) 'The Nature of Plot in Drama' *Essays and Studies*, London: J. Murray, 65–81.

Fletcher, John, and Philip Massinger. *The Sea Voyage* (1622), Literature Online Chadwyck-Healey Database http://lion.chadwyck.co.uk (20 October 2001).

Greene, Robert. *Orlando Furioso* (c1591), Literature Online Chadwyck-Healey Database http://lion.chadwyck.co.uk (20 October 2001).

Hall, Roger T. (1998) *Writing Your First Play*, 2nd ed., Boston, Oxford: Focal Press.

Jones, Emrys (1971) *Scenic Form in Shakespeare*, Oxford: Clarendon Press.

Osolsobě, Ivo (1974) *Divadlo, které mluví, zpívá a tančí* (A Theatre That Speaks, Sings, and Dances), Praha: Editio Supraphon.

Osolsobě, Ivo (1992) *Mnoho povyku pro sémiotiku* (Much Ado About Semiotics), Brno: „G" hudba a divadlo.

The Taming of a Shrew (c. 1594), Literature Online Chadwyck-Healey Database http://lion.chadwyck.co.uk (20 October 2001).

Varela, Francisco J., Evan Thompson, and Eleanor Rosch (1991) *The Embodied Mind: Cognitive Science and Human Experience*, Cambridge, Mass., London: MIT Press.

Wells, Stanley, and Gary Taylor, eds. (1988) *The Oxford Shakespeare: The Complete Works*, Oxford: Clarendon Press.

Zich, Otakar (1931) *Estetika dramatického umění* (Aesthetics of the Dramatic Art), Prague: Melantrich.

12

Pedagogy as Event

A CASE STUDY OF *HAMLET*
AND HAUNTOLOGY

John J. Joughin

Introduction: teaching and criticism

> A performance that repeats itself every evening according to rites that are always the
> same, always identical to what they were the night before, can no longer win our support.
> The spectacle we are watching must be unique, it must give the impression that it is
> unprecedented, as incapable of repeating itself as any action in life, any event brought on by
> circumstances. (Artaud cited in Fortier 1996: 3)

Artaud's comments on theatrical adaptation serve to remind us that staging or setting
always constitutes the 'starting point for theatrical creation' not its end point. By
extending this principle to a teaching situation and speaking of 'pedagogy as event' I
mean to emphasise the way in which teaching and theorising Shakespeare can itself
constitute a form of critical thinking that is creative and open-ended rather than prescriptive or closed. Indeed, I would hope that most teaching like most theorising is
open to 'eventful thinking'.[1] As anyone who has attempted to act in, or direct, or stage-
manage a play knows, the event of drama is often eventful precisely in ways that
allow for contingency and uncertainty. In this respect, claims to knowledge are not
grounded in a fixed or absolute way, but are open to endless contestation and revision.
The analogy with the teaching situation holds if we make the most of an approach to
'education' which relies on an openness to alterity or otherness, in developing a pedagogy that aims to be open to invention and refuses to be prescribed by predetermined
categories. Rather like the relationship between audience and actor, teaching and
learning is always a reciprocal and interactive process, so that critical thinking is

actually a form of shared creative thinking, especially insofar as one learns as much (if not more) as a teacher as one learnt as a student. Like the best nights at the theatre this ensures that, whatever the script, the best seminars are not repeated to 'rites that are always the same', indeed, they 'win our support' by being in some sense unrepeatable.

Of course there are always limits to improvisation; after all, the university seminar is an institution which is bound in certain ways to forms of academic hierarchy and the hegemony of literature imposes constraints of its own. Yet, in a number of ways, the development of literary theory over the last twenty years or so has arguably changed the conditions of teaching by challenging these limitations. The focus on the reader's role in the constitution of meaning, the possibility that texts are open to a number of interpretations, the way in which literature troubles fixed definitions of class, race, gender and sexuality, etc. all offer potential strategies for re-thinking the way in which we deliver Shakespeare courses to undergraduates, as well as helping us to critically re-evaluate some of the presumptions which lie behind our own teaching methods.

Generally speaking this has made for a more reflective and informed approach to teaching. Yet the application of theory can also produce its own form of straitjacket. For one thing, students and lecturers alike are often guilty of recycling theoretical paradigms in a fashion that is restrictive, so that a series of straw targets – humanism, aesthetic value, essentialism – are ritually bowled over according to set criteria. In this respect the academic essay can itself become a form of painting by numbers in which one fixes an interpretative grid to a play and then shades in accordingly. My own practice is to focus on the literary or dramatic text and to stage it as a starting point or a 'score' for interpretation. In practice this often entails interrogating the ways in which this material resists interpretation, or at least confronts us with questions. Hopefully it also serves to remind students that critical issues are in some sense critical precisely because they produce questions rather than answers.

Hauntology

Hence hauntology. The term 'hauntology' is of course borrowed from the French philosopher Jacques Derrida (1994). Derrida's own use of the word produces a pun on 'ontology' – that branch of metaphysics that deals with 'being' and existence, as opposed to that which does not exist. In evoking a sense of the 'non-present present', hauntology might be said to refer to the 'being-there of an absent or departed one' that 'no longer belongs to knowledge' (cf. Derrida 1994: 6). *Hamlet* itself of course opens with the most existential of questions, 'Who's there?'(I.i.1),[2] and in raising the question of identity even before we meet any of the characters, it reminds us in advance of much of that which is to come, insofar as questions concerning ontology – 'To be, or not to be' (III.i.56) etc. – quickly emerge as a crucial motif in the play.

My own interest in running a seminar on hauntology at the very beginning of a

Shakespeare course is that it immediately forces a seminar group to confront the boundaries of their own response. After all, as Derrida's definition suggests, in theorising about a ghost or a 'specter':

> one does not 'know' what it *is*. … *It is* something that one does not know, precisely, and one does not know if precisely it *is*, if it responds to a name and corresponds to an essence. (Derrida 1994: 6).

In confronting an entity that does not fall within conventional bounds of 'naming', one is forced to reconsider 'that which one thinks one knows by the name of knowledge' (6). In dramatic terms of course, the staging of the Ghost in the play allows us to re-evaluate a range of responses in that it not only draws attention to the interaction between 'players and spectators' but also allows us to view players themselves *as* spectators. In practice, discussions concerning hauntology quickly establish a link to that most familiar of strange tropes, the 'uncanny'. As a quick brain-storming session will reveal, most students already have quite a highly developed sense of the uncanny and a rich store of experience relating to the ghostly, déjà vu, strange coincidence, telepathy, etc. Crucially, of course, the uncanny blurs the distinction between 'fictional' and 'lived' experience insofar as life itself is often seen to be stranger than fiction. On the other hand, as Freud himself reminds us, literature is the place where the uncanny features most prevalently.[3] Students have not always considered these phenomena in relation to Shakespeare, yet of course the staging of the Ghost is compelling precisely because it blurs the boundaries between the 'real' and the 'fictional'.

Ghosts feature regularly in Shakespeare and in this respect if we included spirits and other forms of apparition we would be looking at the full range of the playwright's output from *Richard III* and *Julius Caesar* to *A Midsummer Night's Dream* and *The Winter's Tale*, as well as tragedies such as *Hamlet* and *Macbeth*. In the session on *Hamlet*, my approach is to divide the opening scene of the play into manageable segments. In the first instance I present students with three extracts only and ask them to produce a paragraph on each, paying particular attention to issues concerning meaning, timing and staging. Students work in small groups often reading or 're-enacting' first and then discussing in order to reach consensus and report back to the seminar.[4]

Extract one

Enter BARNADO and FRANCISCO, *two* Sentinels.

Bar.	Who's there?
Fran.	Nay, answer me. Stand and unfold yourself.
Bar.	Long live the King!
Fran.	Barnado?

Bar.	He.
Fran.	You come most carefully upon your hour.
Bar.	'Tis now struck twelve. Get thee to bed, Francisco.
Fran.	For this relief much thanks. 'Tis bitter cold,
	And I am sick at heart.
Bar.	Have you had quiet guard?
Fran.	Not a mouse stirring.
Bar.	Well, good night. (I.i.1–12)

Summary of discussion

Getting the students to think about staging is immediately to ask: who says what to whom and from which position? In this respect of course 'Who's there?' (1) already comes from a position offstage, and, as if to invert the 'natural' order of things, we are forced to confront the fact that Barnado's opening question comes from a place 'elsewhere', outside the frame of the play. Even before we get to examine the question of apparition or who can see what, we are aware of someone speaking out of the void enquiring about the identity of another. In some sense then, before we are confronted with the Ghost, we are already presented with an incorporeal presence in the form of a disembodied voice. On working through the implications of this opening line one group suggested that a production could begin with Francisco facing the audience and Barnado asking his question from somewhere in the stalls, thus heightening the sense of being neither quite inside or outside the play at this point. Of course, in terms of its physical location, the scene itself is set on the 'ramparts', although the term 'platform' is also used to describe the setting, a term we now use interchangeably with scaffold or stage.

In turn, Francisco's response to Barnado's enquiry, 'Stand and *unfold* yourself' (2), already directs us to the question of 'exposition' and interpretation, and in doing so it also of course uncannily anticipates the Ghost's repetitive use of the same word 'unfold', during the eventual 'unfolding' of his own tale during I.v. Yet, for the time being, the accent in these opening lines seems to be on the exchange of information and in terms of 'timing' the scene seems orderly enough, this, after all, is a moment of changing the guard, another form of orderly exchange: 'You come most carefully' (6), ''Tis now struck twelve' (7). The emphasis seems to be on punctuality and regimen, yet one of the most perceptive comments I have received on this extract was from a student who reminded the seminar that Barnado's articulation of what is in effect a password, 'Long live the King!' (3), already effectively has a more chilling antecedent silently inscribed alongside it, where the moment of Sovereign succession customarily carries the precursor '*The King is Dead*, Long live the King!'. It is of course a '*pass*word' then in more than one sense. As Dover Wilson long ago commented in his gloss on this line, its inference 'is dramatically ironical in view of all that follows' (i.e. the appearance of a dead King) (Jenkins 1990: 165); we might add that it is doubly ironic in terms of that which comes *before* but is left unarticulated at this point. In syntactical terms at least, another form of absent presence already haunts the play. In interrogating the opening lines of the scene there is already an underlying sense of a strange non-sequential disruption of time – an advance recognition of the past that is both a feature of *Hamlet* and of hauntology more generally.

Extract two

Mar.	Holla, Barnado!
Bar.	Say, what, is Horatio there?
Hor.	A piece of him.
Bar.	Welcome, Horatio. Welcome, good Marcellus.
Hor.	What, has this thing appear'd again tonight?
Bar.	I have seen nothing.
Mar.	Horatio says 'tis but our fantasy,
	And will not let belief take hold of him,
	Touching this dreaded sight twice seen of us.
	Therefore I have entreated him along
	With us to watch the minutes of this night,
	That if again this apparition come,
	He may approve our eyes and speak to it
Hor.	Tush, tush, 'twill not appear. (I.i.20–33)

Summary of discussion

Another scene of 'welcome', though again Horatio's own response to the question of who's there? – 'A piece of him' (21–22) – immediately picks up on the theme of absent presence we have just left behind. In discussing this extract the students quickly realise that there is a lot of speculation here about the 'meaning' of the apparition. Again the fact that this anticipation is about something that has already happened twice before often causes comment. It is, of course, another instance of what theorists would term an untimely or 'achronological' effect, in so far as ghosts' 'comings' and 'goings' refuse to be confined within a sequential or linear narrative, so that as Derrida puts it:

> the spirit comes by coming back [revenant], it figures both a dead man who comes back and a ghost whose expected return repeats itself, again and again. (Derrida 1994: 10)

There is then repetition here but repetition of difference rather than of any*thing* that belongs to the order of the same.

Here again 'speaking' rather than merely 'seeing' arises as a possible means of establishing identity. We learn that Horatio may converse with the spectre or 'speak to *it*'. As the scene unfolds then, the sense of intangibility is becoming more tangible, although the Ghost is still unnamed as such and remains a 'thing' (24), 'a dreaded sight' (28), an 'apparition' (31). For his own part Horatio the sceptic will not credit appearance unless he has the evidence before him. Although Barnado's 'I have seen nothing' (25), whilst ostensibly reporting the non-appearance of the Ghost, is also of course literally what happens when we 'see' a ghost or witness some*thing* that *is*, yet cannot 'be' in any conventional sense.

Extract three

Bar.	Sit down awhile,
	And let us once again assail your ears,
	That are so fortified against our story,
	What we have two nights seen.
Hor.	Well, sit we down.
	And let us hear Barnado speak of this.
Bar.	Last night of all,
	When yond same star that's westward from the pole,
	Had made his course t'illume that part of heaven
	Where it now burns, Marcellus and myself,
	The bell then beating one –

Enter GHOST.

Mar.	Peace, break thee off. Look where it comes again.
Bar.	In the same figure like the King that's dead.
Mar.	Thou art a scholar, speak to it, Horatio.
Bar.	Looks a not like the King? Mark it, Horatio.
Hor.	Most like. It harrows me with fear and wonder.
Bar.	It would be spoke to.
Mar.	Question it Horatio.
Hor.	What art thou that usurp'st this time of night,
	Together with that fair and warlike form
	In which the majesty of buried Denmark
	Did sometimes march? By heaven, I charge thee speak.
Mar.	It is offended.
Bar.	See, it stalks away.
Hor.	Stay, speak, speak, I charge thee speak.
Mar.	'Tis gone and will not answer.

Bar.	How now, Horatio? You tremble and look pale.
	Is not this something more than fantasy?
	What think you on't
Hor.	Before my God, I might not this believe
	Without the sensible and true avouch
	Of mine own eyes.
Mar.	Is it not like the King?
Hor.	As thou art to thyself. (I.i.34–62)

Summary of discussion

This is by far the longest of the three extracts. Yet ending here is a useful way of reminding students that for all the preceding preparation, the Ghost's arrival cannot be prepared for. Indeed, in keeping with the best literary events, 'it' appears quite literally without preamble *in medias res* (into the midst of things), and ironically, in doing so it interrupts Barnado's own 'Ghost story'. Once again, any ordered sense of narrative sequence is made further complicated and the boundary between the 'literary' and the 'fictional' is blurred – as a result the apparition itself is more real than fiction, for as Barnado asks: 'Is not this something more than fantasy?' (57). And again, the apparition is 'thing-like' in that it is referred to as an 'it', although 'it' is used inter-changeably now with the antique form of he ('a') in Barnado's: 'Looks *a* not like the King?' (46). Here and in his preceding observation that the entity appears 'In the same figure like the King that's dead' (44), Barnado relies on a form of recognition that is also a form of *re*-cognition, i.e. a form of cognition that is based on comparison. Marcellus picks up the same comparison moments later, asking Horatio 'Is it not like the King?' (61). Yet Horatio's response to Marcellus, 'As thou art to thyself' (62), teasingly suggests that, insofar as an insistence on simultude or likeness depends upon a sense of difference, then it also constitutes a form of identification that is already split and divided against itself, in that it depends on a self comparing 'self' with self. In another sense, of course, each of the witnesses could be said to be 'beside them-selves' with terror at this point, and in terms of 'staging' we are presented with a set of instructions to the players themselves. Horatio the former sceptic now 'tremble(s) and look(s) pale'(56). Yet by far the most significant feature of this scene for those of us reading for 'meaning' is the quite explicit sense in which it is interpretation that is being called into question here: 'Thou art a scholar, speak to it, Horatio' (46). As Derrida comments:

There has never been a scholar who really, and as a scholar, deals with ghosts. A traditional scholar does not believe in ghosts – nor in all that could be called the virtual space of spectrality. There has never been a scholar who, as such, does not believe in the sharp distinction between the real and the unreal, the actual and the inactual, the living and the non-living, being and non-being. (Derrida 1994: 11)

Horatio's brand of scepticism relies on objective distance and proof and the Ghost is not susceptible to interpretation on these terms. As a consequence, and as a mark of his confusion, the 'scientific' Horatio is now forced to swear a 'religious' oath that he is witnessing something than cannot be, but somehow *is*: 'Before my God, I might not this believe/Without the sensible and true avouch/Of mine own eyes' (59–61).

Hauntology and Theatricality

Aren't all actors just animated corpses anyway, talking animals or ghostly apparitions come to life for the 'two-hours' traffic' of the stage? The finitude of the dramatic performance itself is such that it evokes a lexicon of absent presence – 'we died out there tonight' – so that even when actors fail they refer to it as 'corpsing'. On the other hand, when we refer to the most memorable nights at the theatre we often speak in terms of a 'haunting' performance. Clearly, as Stephen Greenblatt recently reminds us in a book-length study of *Hamlet in Purgatory* (2001), there are 'powerful links between Shakespeare's art and the haunting of spirits'. Indeed, in some ways, as Greenblatt himself suggests, the figure of the ghost in Shakespeare's plays could be taken as 'a figure of theatre' (Greenblatt 2001: 157).

Actually, the session on hauntology constitutes an extremely effective 'prequel' to a follow-up session on the relationship between hauntology and theatricality, and helpfully of course, *Hamlet* itself has a lot to say about the theatre and theatre practice – indeed, it is one of the relatively few sources we have for developing a sense of the contemporary context of early modern theatre and its techniques and conventions. In some sense of course, staging the ghost story is precisely what Hamlet attempts in the play itself insofar as his own attempt to 'test' the accuracy of the Ghost's testimony during the 'mousetrap scene' (III.ii) is founded on a staged adaptation. Moreover the play-within-the-play once again highlights issues relating to interpretation and performance, insofar as it stages an audience on stage and a director (Hamlet) hoping to influence the outcome.

In some respects, of course, Hamlet's problem here is analogous to the problem we have already faced, i.e. how does one stage what is apparently not there? One way of focusing these concerns is to ask the students to reconsider Hamlet's advice to the players (III.ii.1–45) in light of the lessons we learnt about 'apparitions' the preceding week. Now, in contrast, we are confronted with a theatre director (Hamlet) who insists upon a rather naïve sense of the relation between 'theatre' and 'reality'. In advocating a form of mimeticism that would hold the 'mirror up to nature' (22) and a performance that would 'suit the action to the word' (17), Hamlet relies on a rather over-prescriptive sense of the distinction between the real and the unreal. Indeed, he evidently believes that events in a play can be conceived of in terms of their direct correlation to an anterior or predetermined reality, though of course, at the same time, it is precisely the improvisational unexpected 'event-like' nature of theatrical performance that he is forced to concede, complaining that 'clowns' are liable to speak 'more than is set down for them' (39). Actually, then, Hamlet emerges as a rather 'closed' thinker and as such he would prefer to pedantically 'piece out' and over-interpret every aspect of the story, so that as Ophelia observes later on during the scene itself, 'You are as good as a chorus, my Lord' (240).

In some ways Hamlet's failed act of theatrical adaptation (his own attempt to stage the ghost) is seminally instructive for those who attempt to teach theatre in anything other than an open-ended fashion. Whereas the students have questioned the idea of empirical 'evidence' in the first session, Hamlet has not learnt the lesson of hauntology. Nor of course has Horatio, who in preparing to scrutinise Claudius' response to the performance promises Hamlet that (as you would expect from a rational man of science) nothing will escape his 'detecting' (III.ii.89). Unsurprisingly perhaps, many literary critics have repeated the same mistake. In some ways 'the mousetrap' has become the editorial and interpretative crux of the play, and in trying to pin down the 'meaning' of Claudius' response to the play-within-the-play, generations of 'scholars' have effectively committed the same error of attempting to preserve the 'veracity' of the Ghost's testimony 'at all costs'.[5]

This 'forensic' approach to the 'scene of the crime' in Shakespeare's play is nicely parodied in Michael Almereyda's *Hamlet* (2001). The film opens with Ethan Hawke playing the role of Hamlet as a 'video-diarist' who films himself as well as the parts of the play in which he is a character. In the privacy of his own editing suite Hawke then endlessly reviews the footage, an archive that includes excerpts from his own 'Family Album' in which we witness Hamlet Senior embracing Gertrude his wife in happier times (complete with voiceover 'Why she would hang on him/As if increase of appetite had grown/By what it fed on …' (I.ii.143–5)), as well as shots of Ophelia, and yet the cumulative effect of this video 'evidence' only increases Hamlet's doubt. Here, in a multimedia society, too much rather than too little information is the problem. As if to emphasise the point, the Ghost is first spotted on security cameras haunting the subterranean depths of the *Denmark Corporation*. Yet the spectral grainy image of the CCTV only reminds us of the uncertainty of being. Rather like the last moments of Diana leaving the Hotel Ritz in Paris, the allusion here seems to be to the impossibility of ever witnessing the scene of the 'crime'; we are left instead with an iconography of absence, a message Almereyda emphasises by Hawke constantly reviewing the video image of himself holding a gun to his head whilst reciting the 'To be or not to be' soliloquy. In attempting to pluck out the heart of the mystery digital information leaves us with evidence of a kind, but however we attempt to edit the sequence of events or capture their significance, the 'event' itself remains inexplicable and haunting. In the process, whether Hamlet is cast as a theatre theorist or video director, insofar as he's a master of the media, he remains a poor judge of the event of drama itself.

Conclusion

I have tried to suggest the various ways in which issues surrounding 'hauntology' alert students to the fact that an engagement with a literary or dramatic text is not so much a matter of recognition, but rather a matter of re-cognition – where the emphasis falls on the re, the comparative and evaluative axis by which we return to encounter a text in new ways. Critical thinking is reflective thinking, and while recent theoretical approaches to literature have conceded the fact that literary texts transform meaning and are open to a variety of interpretations, they have rather shied away from asking precisely how these revelations are to be understood. Such moments could conceivably be construed purely in formal or 'linguistic terms', in relation to overturning conventional expectations or in breaking with existing rules. Yet the revelatory potential of aesthetic disclosure needs to be understood as a more participatory and consensual event, in the course of which, as Andrew Bowie puts it, in defamiliarising habitual perceptions, 'something comes to be seen as something in a new way' (Bowie 1997: 301).[6]

This arguably takes us into the area of literary judgement and evaluation, yet in practice this type of discussion need not be cast according to more functional or prescriptive senses of high versus low culture. For one thing, *Hamlet* itself collapses these very boundaries; after all the postmodern Gothic pastiche of the graveyard scene V.i. is not so far removed from the irreverent mirth of *Buffy the Vampire Slayer*. Yet students' recognition that this is so simultaneously depends on a sophisticated sense of comparison that has everything to do with an appreciation of the difference. In a more fundamental sense of course the very idea of 'play' is itself directly implicated in precisely this type of cognitive negotiation, in that, as Isobel Armstrong reminds us:

> Play achieves an extraordinary reversal, a transformation of the very structure of perception. … play is liberating through its capacity to be interactive: because the child can create an alienated meaning within the constraints of a specific, concrete situation, play occupies 'the realm of spontaneity and freedom'. (Armstrong 2000: 38)

Tied to actuality, in ways that cannot be reduced to the empirical or verifiable, the experience of 'play' allows instead for the creation of new 'possible worlds'. And what else, we might ask, should educators be doing if not allowing for the possibility of precisely these forms of transformation?[7]

In the course of provoking thought and in making us think again, literary texts could themselves be construed as 'phantoms' – traces of memory that provoke thought, yet continue to resist any definitive critical appropriation. After all, how can we 'know' that which simultaneously remains beyond our full comprehension? Or even (as Marcellus requires of the scholar Horatio) 'speak to it'? Does this apparently irreducible capacity for reinvention, in turn, leave us with a Shakespeare which is 'for all time'? Well perhaps, though as Derrida reminds us, hauntology is historical only insofar as it resists a unilinear account of history:

> haunting is historical, to be sure, but it is not *dated*, it is never docilely given a date in the chain of presents, day after day, according to the instituted order of a calendar. (Derrida 1994: 4, original italics)

Rather like the logic of haunting, the survival of Shakespeare inside and outside the classroom is caught up in a process which is interruptive, untimely and out-of-joint. This means that each encounter is singular, always a first time as well as a last time (cf. Derrida 1994: 10). In this sense at least, then, teaching and theorising Shakespeare cannot be part of some universal or 'never-ending' process. Indeed, for most of us it can only ever be said to have just begun.

Notes

1   I owe the term 'eventful thinking' to Thomas Docherty (forthcoming 2003) who coins the expression to signify thinking which is eventful 'precisely to the extent that its outcome cannot be predetermined'.

2   All references to *Hamlet* are taken from Jenkins 1990.

3   See Freud 1963. I should note a long-term indebtedness here to the extremely accessible introduction to 'The Uncanny' provided by Bennett and Royle 1999: 36–43, which is designed to cater for undergraduates and which I would thoroughly recommend.

4   In what follows I will be rehearsing a composite narrative culled at random from various sessions. I suppose it could stand as a case study insofar as a case study conflates the evidence and imposes its own narrative. It is then, in some sense, a form of generalisation or summary. Need I add that any resemblance to individuals alive or dead is entirely coincidental?

5   I owe this point to Stanley Cavell 1987: 181.

6   For a more detailed consideration of aesthetic disclosure in relation to Shakespeare, see Joughin 2000.

7   I am indebted to Thomas Docherty for highlighting this connection between play and aesthetic education see his 'Aesthetic education and the demise of experience' (Docherty, *forthcoming* 2003).

References

Armstrong, I. (2000) *The Radical Aesthetic*, Oxford: Blackwell.

Artaud, A. (1988) *Selected Writings*, Berkeley: University of California Press.

___ (1989) 'The Theatre of Cruelty: First Manifesto', *The Theatre and its Double*, trans. V. Corti, London: John Calder, 68–78.

Bennett, A. and Royle, N. (1999) *An Introduction to Literature, Criticism and Theory*, Hemel Hempstead: Prentice Hall Europe.

Bowie, A. (1997) *From Romanticism to Critical Theory: The Philosophy of German Literary Theory*, London and New York: Routledge.

Cavell, S. (1987) *Disowning Knowledge: In Six Plays of Shakespeare*, Cambridge: Cambridge University Press.

Derrida, J. (1994) *Specters of Marx: the state of the debt, the work of mourning, and the new international*, trans. P. Kamuf, London and New York: Routledge.

Docherty, Thomas (*forthcoming* 2003) 'Aesthetic education and the demise of experience', Joughin, J. and Malpas, S. (eds), *The New Aestheticism*, Manchester: Manchester University Press.

Freud, S. (1963) 'The Uncanny', Strachey, J. ed. *Complete Psychological Works*, vol. XVII, London: Standard Edition, 217–56.

Fortier, M.(1996) 'Shakespeare as "Minor Theatre": Deluze and Guattari and the Aims of Adaptation' *Mosaic* 29.1: 1–18.

Garber, M. (1987) *Shakespeare's Ghost Writers*, London and New York: Methuen.

Greenblatt, S. J. (2001) *Hamlet in Purgatory*, Princeton, N.J.: Princeton University Press.

Hawkes, T. (1986) *That Shakespeherian Rag: Essays on a Critical Process*, London and New York: Methuen.

Holderness, G. (1987) *Hamlet*, Milton Keynes: Open University Press.

Jenkins, H. (ed.) (1990) *Hamlet*, London: Routledge.

Joughin, J. J. (2000) 'Shakespeare, modernity and the aesthetic: Art, truth and judgement in *The Winter's Tale*', Grady, H. (ed), *Shakespeare and Modernity: Early Modern to Millennium*, London and New York: Routledge.

Contributors

Paromita Chakravarti is a lecturer in English literature at Jadavpur University, Kolkata, India. She is completeing her doctoral thesis on Renaissance folly at St Catherine's College, University of Oxford. She has been a Radhakrishnan scholar and a Violet Vaughan Morgan scholar at Oxford. Apart from the Renaissance, she is also interested in women's writing, Gender studies and film and media studies. She has participated in seminars and lectured and written on these topics at Indian universities and abroad.

Mary T. Christel has been teaching world literature, drama, and media studies at Adlai E. Stevenson High School in the United States for the past 23 years as well as teaching courses in Shakespeare and cinema studies for gifted adolescents at Northwestern University. She has contributed to *Teaching Shakespeare Today* (National Council of Teachers of English) and *Teaching Shakespeare into the 21st Century* (University of Ohio Press) and co-authored *Seeing and Believing: How to Teach Media Literacy in the English Classroom* (Heinemann). In 1998, she was a co-chair for the 2nd International Conference on Shakespeare sponsored by the National Council of Teachers of English.

Pavel Drábek is assistant lecturer at the Department of English and American Studies, Faculty of Arts, Masaryk University, Brno, Czech Republic. Currently he is finishing his doctoral studies at Charles University, Prague, having written a thesis on mature drama by John Fletcher and his collaborators called *Fletcherian Dramatic Achievement*. His other work includes translations of medieval and early modern texts into Czech, and mini-opera projects.

Swati Ganguly is a senior lecturer in English literature at Visva–Bharati University, Santiniketan. She is currently working on the Renaissance grotesque. Her interests include women's writing, translation studies, theatre and visual arts. A practicing translator, she has been a Charles Wallace fellow for translation studies and was a translator in residence at BCLT, UEA, Norwich, UK. She has co-edited and translated a collection of Bengali women's fiction. Ms Ganguly is also a creative writer in Bengali and a collection of her short stories has been published recently.

Mark Houlahan teaches Renaissance studies and theory in the English Department of the University of Waikato, Hamilton, New Zealand. His essay for this volume is part of his ongoing research into the place of Shakespeare in post-colonial cultures like his own.

Kay D. Johnston is an Associate Professor of Educational Studies at Colgate University, New York. Her interests include moral development and teacher education.

John J. Joughin is Reader in English Literature in the Department of Cultural Studies, University of Central Lancashire, UK. He is editor of *Shakespeare and National Culture* (Manchester: Manchester University Press, 1997) and *Philosophical Shakespeares* (London and New York: Routledge, 2000).

Margaret Maurer is a Professor of English at Colgate University, New York, and has been involved in the Teaching Shakespeare Institute at the Folger Shakespeare Library.

Mary Janell Metzger teaches Shakespeare as well as critical theory and women's literature at Western Washington University in Bellingham, Washington.

Roger Ochse teaches Shakespeare and technical communication at Black Hills State University (USA). Currently, he is writing a book about teaching Shakespeare in a digital age, based on his experience with computer technology and his participation in an international institute at the reconstructed Blackfriars Playhouse in Staunton, Virginia, and at Shakespeare's Globe Theatre in London.

Derek Peat worked for over twenty-five years in various positions at the University of Sydney, but in 1999, when he was Director of Marketing, he felt he had had more than enough and took voluntary redundancy. He now works happily as a teacher of English at Blue Mountains Grammar School in Wentworth Falls, New South Wales, where he also manages the Library.

Catherine Silverstone is currently completing a DPhil thesis on Shakespeare and performance at the University of Sussex. She has taught courses on Shakespeare and early modern drama at universities in New Zealand and the United Kingdom.

Paul Skrebels is a Senior Lecturer in Professional Writing and Communication in the School of Communication, Information and New Media, University of South Australia. He has produced articles, chapters and conference presentations internationally on cultural and writerly approaches to teaching and studying Shakespeare.

Ted Tibbetts teaches English and Shakespeare at Portland High School in Portland, Maine. He also serves as a faculty adviser for a high school Shakespearean acting troupe. A Russell Award winner, Maine Teacher of the Year State Finalist, and Milken Family Foundation Award winner, he has presented Shakespeare Workshops around the United States.

Sieta van der Hoeven currently tutors in Professional Writing and Communication in the School of Communication, Information and New Media, University of South Australia. She has recently submitted her doctoral thesis on the use of the adolescent fiction novel in secondary English classes. Before that she was an English teacher.

Acknowledgements

The editors would like to thank the following people for their help and kindness in the process of assembling this collection: John Bell and Gill Perkins of the Bell Shakespeare Company; Robyn Cations of AATE; Michael Bollen of Wakefield Press; and finally, the contributors themselves, without whose enthusiastic and erudite response to our call for papers, their readiness to amend and negotiate at short notice, and the huge amount of cumulative experience and learning their chapters represent, this book would obviously not have been possible.

Index